Darcie A. MacMahon and William H. Marquardt

THE
CALUSA
AND THEIR LEGACY

South Florida People and Their Environments

University Press of Florida
Gainesville · Tallahassee · Tampa · Boca Raton
Pensacola · Orlando · Miami · Jacksonville · Ft. Myers

Copyright 2004 by Darcie A. MacMahon and William H. Marquardt
Printed in Canada on acid-free paper

19 18 17 16 15   6 5 4 3 3 2

A record of cataloging-in-publication data is available from the Library of Congress.
ISBN 0-8130-2773-X

Frontispiece: Tableau depicting the interior of a Calusa leader's house.
Photo by Tammy Johnson.

The University Press of Florida is the scholarly publishing agency for the State University System of Florida, comprising Florida A&M University, Florida Atlantic University, Florida Gulf Coast University, Florida International University, Florida State University, University of Central Florida, University of Florida, University of North Florida, University of South Florida, and University of West Florida.

University Press of Florida
15 Northwest 15th Street
Gainesville, FL 32611-2079
http://www.upf.com

Contents

16. Seminole and Miccosukee Culture and Arts 150

17. The Future of South Florida 163

Foreword

In the early 1980s archaeologist William H. Marquardt returned to his native Florida to join the curatorial staff at the Florida Museum of Natural History. We are very glad he did.

A veteran of field research in the southwestern United States and the Archaic period shell mounds of Kentucky, as well as sites in Georgia, South Carolina, and Missouri, Bill also has published on archaeological work in France. After New Mexico and Burgundy, could he find happiness back in Florida? Yes, indeed he can.

Since 1983, Bill has directed an interdisciplinary archaeological project investigating the Calusa Indian people of southwest Florida and their precolumbian ancestors. Deftly combining the efforts of historians, field archaeologists, environmental archaeologists, teachers, and a host of other specialists, including modern-day fisherfolk, he has fashioned an extraordinarily successful research and education enterprise, one which has a permanent presence in the guise of the Randell Research Center, a facility located in Pineland, Lee County. Were there Calusa alive today, I am certain Bill Marquardt would be made an honorary member.

Another native Floridian and honorary Calusa—I see her as one of those powerful women leaders who were prominent in the precolumbian southeast United States—is my colleague Darcie A. MacMahon, the senior author of this volume. An archaeologist, museum specialist, and Tai Chi instructor, Darcie has brought new ideas and considerable skills to the Florida Museum of Natural History. Together, she and Bill have produced a host of popular educational materials—including a video—to inform the public about the Calusa. Perhaps most notably, they also assembled a team headed by Darcie to create a state-of-the art museum exhibit in Gainesville at the Florida Museum of Natural History (www.flmnh.ufl.edu). The Hall of South Florida People and Environments opened to rave reviews in October 2002. It is one of the most spectacular museum displays I have ever seen, and the exhibits reflect Darcie's prowess as a creator of engaging exhibits.

The Calusa and Their Legacy: South Florida People and Their Environments takes the research of the southwest Florida project and combines it with the educational acumen of the exhibit to produce the first popular book focusing on the Calusa, their ancestors, and the coastal water world in which they lived. It also takes a look at the arts and culture of contemporary south Florida Indian people—the Seminoles and Miccosukees. This wonderfully illustrated volume is a delightful rendering of one of the truly unique archaeological and natural areas in the Americas. Anyone interested in North American Indian people, Florida, and the natural history of coastal environments of yesterday and today will love this book.

It is a joy to have such accomplished colleagues, and I am pleased they chose to publish their book in the Native People, Cultures, and Places of the Southeastern United States series. Thanks, Darcie and Bill.

Jerald T. Milanich
Series Editor

Acknowledgments

This book was inspired by the Hall of South Florida People and Environments, a permanent exhibition at the Florida Museum of Natural History in Gainesville. Planning and fabrication of this award-winning exhibition were funded in part by major gifts and grants from the Florida Department of State—Division of Historical Resources, the National Endowment for the Humanities, the Jessie Ball duPont Foundation, the State of Florida Matching Gifts Trust Fund, the Ruth and Vernon Taylor Foundation, David and Mary Ann Cofrin, Anina Hills Glaize, the Raymond Stober family, the New York Times Foundation, and the Florida Legislature.

The research on which this book and the exhibit were based was supported by the National Endowment for the Humanities, the National Science Foundation, the Knight Foundation, the Florida Department of State—Division of Historical Resources, the Ruth and Vernon Taylor Foundation, the Maple Hill Foundation, the Wentworth Foundation, the Florence Dewey White Foundation, the Calusa Constituency, and the volunteer time of many individuals in southwest Florida.

Many people contributed to this book and to the exhibition on which it is based, including colleagues both within and outside the Florida Museum of Natural History. We would especially like to thank Kurt Auffenberg, Stan Blomeley, Jason Bourque, Stacey Breheny, Nathan Bruce, George Burgess, Betty Camp, Brian Chamberlain, Ron Chesser, Merald Clark, Dorr Dennis, Bob Edic, Jon Fajans, Jay Fowler, Dick Franz, Jeff Gage, Dana Griffin, Joan Herrera, Rosalyn Howard, Cherry Johnson, Dale Johnson, Tom Kyne, Bob Leavy, Elise LeCompte, Roger Mallot, Frank Maturo, Scott Mitchell, Clay Montague, Ben Olaivar, Pat Payne, Roger Portell, Irv Quitmyer, Rob Robins, Jack Rudloe, Charles Tompkins, Karen Walker, Tom Webber, Terry Weik, John Worth, and the Special Collections Library at the University of Florida for their invaluable assistance. Many of Merald Clark's excellent drawings reconstructing Calusa life appear in both the exhibit and this book.

We would also like to thank the Native American consultants who worked with us on the exhibition and who thus contributed to this book. We worked most closely with Billy Cypress (now deceased), executive director of the Seminole Tribal Museum Authority and Mikasuki speaker from the Hollywood Reservation; Mary Frances Johns (now deceased), a Mikasuki-speaking Seminole from the Brighton Reservation; Madelaine Tongkeamha, a Creek-speaking Seminole from the Brighton Reservation; and Joe Quetone, director of the Florida Governor's Council on Indian Affairs. Many other Seminole and Miccosukee people contributed to the project, which has benefited greatly from their participation. Especially helpful were Henry John Billie, James Billie, Sonny Billie, William Cypress, Ronnie Jimmie, Sylvester Jimmie, Martha Jones, Jerica Sanders, and Samuel Tommie.

We appreciate the insightful and constructive suggestions of Meredith Morris-Babb and John Byram of the University Press of Florida, series editor Jerald Milanich, and reviewers Carol Newcomb-Jones and Brent Weisman. Joan Herrera, Clay Montague, and Jack Rudloe also reviewed the biology of the natural science stories. All of their opinions have helped shape this book.

The information in the book relies on and summarizes the works of many scholars. Although not footnoted directly in the text, these sources are listed in the bibliography. We greatly appreciate their contributions and hope that we have done them justice in our brief summaries. Any errors and omissions are strictly those of the authors.

ⓑⓑⓑⓑⓑⓑ

South Florida People
and Their Environments

This book is focused on the Calusa, a fascinating but little-known Native American people who controlled the southern peninsula of Florida when Europeans first arrived (figure 1.1). It is also about the rich environment that has supported the Calusa and other people for thousands of years. Indeed, the story of the Calusa cannot be told properly without understanding the coastal environment that they called home. The rich blue-green waters of southwest Florida's estuaries—places where fresh water from the land meets and mixes with salt water of the ocean—provided the Calusa with such abundance that they thrived for many centuries without ever needing to farm.

By the 1760s the Calusa had disappeared from Florida; but the fishing tradition continued: first with Spanish Cubans working with Indian people, later with American fisherfolk. In this book we describe some of these people and their fishing strategies and reflect on the continuity of the fishing tradition on Florida's Gulf coast.

Indian people live in south Florida today, although they are not related to the Calusa. The Seminoles and Miccosukees have vibrant modern cultures, yet they maintain many of their ancient traditions. This book tells their story too.

Who Were the Calusa?

The Calusa were the last native Florida Indian people to succumb to the European invasion and colonization that followed Christopher Columbus's first landing in the New World. From their homeland on the coast of southwest Florida, they exerted influence as far away as today's Cape Canaveral and received tribute—a payment of goods or services to show loyalty to a political leader—from as far away as Lake Okeechobee, present-day Miami, and the Florida Keys (figure 1.2).

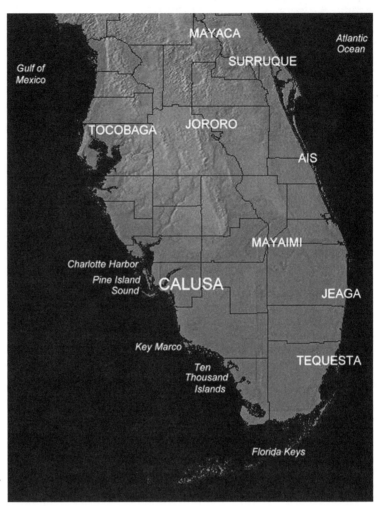

Figure 1.1. South Florida, showing native cultural groups in south Florida and some present-day locations. (Map by John Worth.)

In the 1560s, the Calusa domain itself included at least fifty villages; and by 1612 Spanish governor Juan Fernández de Olivera reported that the Calusa leader controlled "more than sixty villages of his own, not to mention the other very great quantity that pay tribute to him" (Hann 1991).

Central to the Calusa domain was Charlotte Harbor, near present-day Fort Myers (plate 1). Fresh water from the Peace, Myakka, and Caloosahatchee rivers, the protection provided by coastal barrier islands, and a shallow, grassy estuary of extraordinary year-round productivity contributed to Calusa success at fishing and shellfish gathering.

From the estuary, the Calusa harvested over fifty fish species and more than twenty kinds of mollusks and crustaceans. They ate shellfish, crabs, land and aquatic turtles, ducks, deer, rodents, and other animals; but fish were the main staple food. The Calusa most commonly ate pinfish, pigfish, and catfish.

The Calusa and Their Legacy

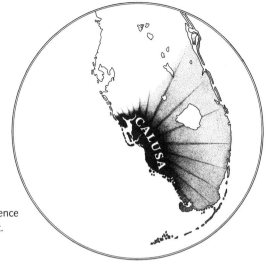

Figure 1.2. Area of Calusa influence at the time of European contact. (Drawing by Merald Clark.)

The Calusa used numerous plants for food, medicine, and fuel. Among these were the saw-palmetto berry, cabbage palm, cocoplum, seagrape, pond apple, mastic, hog plum, acorn, goosefoot, sea purslane, prickly pear cactus fruit, grape, chile pepper, hackberry, water lily, rhizome, and tuber. They obtained fuel from mangrove, buttonwood, pine, red cedar, and wax myrtle trees. The Calusa depended on plants to provide raw materials for tools, handles, containers, clothing, thatching, mats, weapons, canoes, fishing gear, and cordage for the all-important nets. They used gourds as containers and net floats. They probably cultivated gourd-like squash and papaya by about 2,000 years ago, but there is no evidence for large-scale agriculture or any dependence on staple crops.

The Calusa made fishing gear such as sinkers, net weights, net-mesh gauges, and anchors from robust mollusk shells and made hammering, pounding, perforating, and cutting tools from lightning whelks, horse conchs, and other mollusk shells. They used deer bones to make pins, points, fishing gorges, and parts of compound fishhooks, and antlers to make handles. The Calusa created beads from shells and certain bird bones and shaped turtle carapaces into net-mesh gauges. They used shark teeth for grating, cutting, carving, and engraving (plate 2).

From wood and fiber the Calusa built fish traps, weirs, and corrals. They carved wood into bowls, boxes, planks, canoes, paddles, and pounding and grinding implements as well as a wide range of ceremonial and decorative items, such as masks, ear ornaments, and figurines. Natural dyes, latex, and oils were used to make paints for decorating art objects as well as their bodies. They made utilitarian pottery for cooking and storage out of clay and sand.

The Calusa constructed their wood and palm-thatch houses on mounds and ridges of seashells and soil, called *middens*. At least some people lived in large communal thatched houses. In the 1690s there were sixteen such houses in the main Calusa village, each apparently accommodating several dozen people.

Both men and women wore only the briefest hide or mat coverings. They took personal adornment seriously, however. Body paint was common, especially on ritual occasions, and had spiritual significance. In 1568 Spanish Jesuit missionary Juan Rogel noted that the Calusa leader wore his hair long and stained his face and his body black. Commenting on events in the Florida Keys in 1743, Joseph Javier Alaña and Joseph María wrote that "the men paint themselves variously almost every day, a custom they practice, we have learned, for the honor of the principal idol that they venerate" (Hann 1991).

European observers noted that the Calusa were divided into nobles and commoners. The nobles did not work; nor did warriors at the command of the Calusa leader. Nobles had access to certain foods denied to commoners, and spiritual specialists and healers received special treatment and compensation for their services.

The paramount leader (*cacique*) sat on a special stool. He and his sons were fanned with incense by the chief priest. The leader received tribute from town chiefs, but in turn he distributed to them some of the goods salvaged from Spanish shipwrecks. Each town loyal to the Calusa leader provided him a bride. Although the leaders were usually men, Spaniard Hernando de Escalante Fontaneda made reference to a female leader (*cacica*) in one description of sacrifices and rituals among the Calusa.

The paramount, a military captain, and a spiritual leader were the three primary officials. Calusa people believed that their paramount leader mediated between the secular and sacred realms, so they equated his health and prosperity with their own. The "Great Captain," or chief military leader, waged war on behalf of the Calusa and commanded military specialists and a militia that could be mobilized at the request of the paramount leader. The paramount could also command that subjects in all the towns under his control manufacture weapons to meet a threat. The spiritual leader maintained the temple and its idols, was believed to have the power to summon storms, and probably coordinated or conducted important rites of passage, including death rituals and human sacrifice.

The Calusa buried their dead in mounds or cemeteries. They feared the dead and placed food, herbs, and tobacco offerings for the departed on mats at the burial places. Skulls of animals (such as stags, turtles, and barracudas) were also placed at gravesites. The Calusa consulted their dead ancestors in order to foretell the future or to learn of happenings in other places.

European-introduced diseases, militarism, slavery, and displacement eventually took their toll. By 1711 the remaining Calusa had been enslaved, killed, or driven from their homeland. Some lived for a time in the Florida

Keys, under continuing pressure from Indian slavers working for English colonists. Spaniards living in Cuba rescued some of the south Florida Indian people, but most died of typhus and smallpox soon after reaching Cuba. Among the deceased were the paramount leader and military leader of the Calusa. A few south Florida Indians went to Cuba in 1760. Calusa society fades from the historical record in the eighteenth century.

How Do We Know about the Past?

Documents pertaining to south Florida native people were written by Europeans—Spanish, French, and English strangers in what for them was a bizarre world of unfamiliar animals, plants, and people. Although the Calusa and other south Florida natives had a rich heritage of language and arts, they left no written records. The writings that we have reflect European perceptions and sensibilities, not those of the native people.

Until 1895 the documents were all we had. But in April of that year a chance find of carved wood, fiber, and shell artifacts in a mucky area on Key Marco (now called Marco Island), Florida, led to the discovery of one of the most remarkable archaeological sites ever investigated. When Smithsonian anthropologist Frank Cushing saw the objects, he immediately made plans for an expedition. Over a five-week period, he and his assistants unearthed objects of shell, bone, fired clay, antler, wood, and fiber, preserved perfectly in the oxygen-free conditions of the Marco Island muck (figure 1.3). These items included fishing nets with their wooden floats and clam-shell weights

Figure 1.3. Field photograph of the Key Marco site during excavations in 1896. (Courtesy of Smithsonian Institution, National Anthropological Archives.)

still attached, carved and painted wooden masks, and intricately sculpted wooden human and animal figurines.

Strictly speaking, the Key Marco site on Marco Island lies at the extreme south of the Calusa region in the Ten Thousand Islands area occupied historically by the Muspa. Muspa-area pottery and other artifact styles were distinct from those in the Calusa heartland until about A.D. 1300, when they became very similar throughout southwest Florida. Thus it is likely that the Muspa were allied with the Calusa and probably under their control within the last two centuries before European contact. We include the Key Marco finds in our discussion of the Calusa.

Frank Cushing was one of the brightest and most accomplished scholars of American Indian culture of his time, but the archaeology of that period would be considered haphazard and irresponsible today. Brightly colored masks and painted boxes faded upon contact with the air. Beautiful carved and painted items fell apart when removed from the watery environment where they had been buried for centuries. Today's conservators have developed techniques that would allow such items to be preserved.

In contrast to their nineteenth-century predecessors, today's archaeologists are just as concerned with mundane items such as fish bones, seeds, and undecorated pottery as they are with splendid art objects. By studying the small details found in the garbage heaps, or middens, we come to understand the daily lives of past people and the natural environment in which they lived.

As in Cushing's day, the *context* of the find—its surroundings and what it is associated with—is as important as the find itself. Items that are found close together may have been used together (giving us a clue to their functions) and can generally be considered to date to the same time in the past. If an object of unknown age is found in context with an object of known age, the mystery object is probably about the same age as the known item.

When we put all the puzzle pieces together, we learn something about past people and sometimes about ourselves. Today's archaeologists are often anthropologists. Anthropologists believe that as we learn about a particular group of people we also learn something about all people. In this book you will learn about the Calusa, their neighbors, their way of life, their surroundings, and the people who came after them.

Knowing about Florida's heritage and environment is important. Estuaries, rivers, and seacoasts of south Florida that have supported people for literally thousands of years still nurture and protect us today. But those environments are deteriorating—even the oceans. The historical perspectives we gain by doing archaeology, studying history, and talking to our elders all point to the same conclusion. We cannot afford the luxury of leaving environmental knowledge to a few specialists. As a society, we must gain a better

Figure 1.4. As archaeologists learn new insights about the past, they teach them to the next generation. Here school-children tour excavations at the Pineland site in southwest Florida. (Photo by William Marquardt.)

appreciation of how our environment works for us, so that as individuals we can work to assure that it is here for us and our children tomorrow.

Today's fishing nets function much like those of the Calusa, and people enjoy the beauty of south Florida coastlines much as the Calusa must have. Sport fishers still delight in catching redfish and seatrout, and millions enjoy shrimp and oysters. In this book we pass on some of what we have learned about the Calusa and the environment that supported them in southwest Florida. We also discuss others who came after them—Cuban fishing people of the 1700s, Seminoles and others in the 1800s, and commercial and sport fishers of the 1900s. We hope to convey an appreciation both for the diverse cultures that have preceded us and for those living in south Florida today. Understanding the past and how it has influenced the present will help us to make better decisions for the future (figure 1.4).

One of the ways to appreciate past Floridians is to study their *artifacts*— the objects they left behind. Most of the artifacts shown in this book are from the collections of the Florida Museum of Natural History, and many of those pictured are on exhibit in the Hall of South Florida People and Environments at the museum on the University of Florida campus in Gainesville. We have also chosen to include images of some of the more remarkable objects held by other institutions.

But the artifacts left by the Calusa are only part of the story. Their environment, the estuary, was fundamental to their success. Before we look closely at the Calusa themselves, we need to understand how the mangroves, sea grasses, mudflats, and water fit together to make up the estuarine system, which provided a bountiful supply of food that supported the Calusa for many centuries.

2

〰〰〰〰〰〰

The Estuary

Cradle of the Ocean

The world of the Calusa was sustained by the rich bounty of the estuary (plate 3). Estuaries are essential to the Calusa story. The enormous success of their society—politically powerful, socially complex, and artistically sophisticated—cannot truly be understood without appreciating estuaries. These people depended on their environment for their prosperity and for their inspiration. Looking at artifacts and historical documents is one way of understanding the Calusa and their neighbors, but learning why estuaries are such rich environments adds an important dimension to our understanding of human success in south Florida over thousands of years. When we look closely at estuaries, we also realize how they are important to us today.

What are estuaries? An estuary is a body of water where fresh water flowing off the land meets and mixes with salt water of the sea, producing one of the earth's richest and most productive environments. Estuaries are often called "cradles of the ocean," because many fish and shellfish develop there early in life, and some spend all of their lives there (figure 2.1).

All sorts of fascinating organisms live in estuaries, interact with each other, and create this productive environment. Surely the Calusa came to know and appreciate them in great detail. They especially understood the organisms that they depended on for food and raw materials and the others that they honored in ornamental carvings and paintings. Even organisms that were unknown to the Calusa, such as the billions of tiny microorganisms that support the food web, were also fundamental to their success.

Estuaries are important to us today just as they were important to the Calusa:

- A healthy estuary produces four to ten times the organic matter produced by a cultivated cornfield of the same size. Although not eaten directly by humans, this organic matter contributes to a diverse and flourishing food web.

- Many species of marine fish and shellfish, including more than ninety percent of those we eat, depend on estuaries at some point during their development.
- Countless fish, birds, mammals, and other wildlife depend on estuaries for food and shelter.
- Estuarine soils, grasses, and tree roots absorb the energy from storm surges and help protect towns.
- On a less mundane—but no less important—level, estuaries are good for the soul. They are beautiful places to visit and enjoy (as many boaters, bird-watchers, and photographers well know), and plenty of discoveries await beachcombers and snorkelers.

Estuaries never stop moving and changing. Once or twice daily, the incoming tide turns land into water, submerging plants and flooding creeks, marshes, and mudflats. Aquatic animals that have sought refuge in the mud emerge into the rising tide. Fish come closer to shore in search of food. Wad-

Figure 2.1. Game fish, such as this snook caught by fisherman Scott Mitchell, depend on healthy estuaries for survival. The snook was released unharmed just after the photo was taken. (Photo by John Worth.)

Figure 2.2. Location of Florida's estuaries. (Graphic by Merald Clark.)

ing birds flock in to hunt for fish, worms, crabs, and clams. Then the tide recedes again, the fish retreat to deeper waters, and the land reappears. On a smaller scale, huge quantities of microscopic plants and animals (phytoplankton and zooplankton) anchor the foundation of the marine food web, and countless billions of bacteria constantly work to process decaying plants and animals in a grand, natural recycling system that never ends.

Estuaries are a paradox. On one hand, there are risks to survival at this interface of land and sea. The estuary is in flux, as the tides roll in and out, as land is exposed and inundated, and as the levels of fresh water and salt water change. The animals and plants that live there must be able to withstand constantly changing temperature, salinity, and water level. On the other hand, estuaries are some of the most productive ecosystems on earth, supplying huge amounts of foodstuffs for innumerable life forms. The nooks and crannies among the mangrove roots and sea grass beds also create impenetrable hiding places for small animals and juvenile fish. In the end, the benefits outweigh the risks and challenges for the many species that call the estuary home.

Estuaries occur throughout the world wherever salt water meets fresh water. With Florida's extensive coastline, this means that large and small estuaries occur throughout the state's coastal zone (figure 2.2). The Calusa heartland was centered on the large estuary at Charlotte Harbor, near present-day Fort Myers, and from there southward to the Ten Thousand Islands. Let's take a closer look at the estuary that was home to the remarkable Calusa people. We'll look at the big picture and then start at the bottom in the mud and work our way up.

The Calusa and Their Legacy

᭞᭞᭞᭞᭞᭞

What Is a Food Web?

All living things in the estuary are connected to one another in what is aptly called a "food web." The image of a web reminds us of the vital connection between energy and all forms of life. Plants store energy from the sun in their leaves, stems, and roots. Animals do not make their own food, so they depend on plants directly or indirectly for energy. Some animals eat plants, and other animals eat animals, passing along the sun's stored energy that plants have captured. A "recycling crew" of insects, bacteria, fungi, and other organisms consumes dead animals and plants and again makes nutrients available for others. All of these links form a food web. Humans are part of the estuarine food web, too, because we consume the fish and shellfish that depend on the estuary for their existence.

᭞᭞᭞᭞᭞᭞

3

⑥⑥⑥⑥⑥⑥⑥

What's the Big Picture?

When most of us think of natural areas, we visualize trees and plants, the sky, perhaps some animals, and the colors, sounds, and smells. From our time spent swimming, boating, or walking along shorelines, we may think of dolphins, manatees, fish, and pretty shells. Rarely do we consider the huge array of life forms that make up natural systems. Often they are hard to see, and there is little opportunity to view them up close. Yet the things we do see are supported by a large system of organisms that remain elusive or invisible to the eye. Everything is connected and depends on other parts of the system to remain alive.

Let's take an unlikely example—animal feces or "poop." Who likes feces? Well, what may look like crab feces to you and me (and the Calusa) looks like food to all sorts of bacteria, plankton, and many animals. The feces of crabs, worms, clams, and other estuarine dwellers are an important part of the food web. They fertilize the soil for plants such as sea grasses and become food for the many tiny organisms that sustain the estuarine food web.

We can't stop there. Here are a few more enticing examples of interconnections in the estuary.

Abundant Plankton

Plankton are another estuary "secret"—easily overlooked by the casual visitor, but a vital food source for enormous numbers of estuarine dwellers. These mostly microscopic animals (zooplankton) and plants (phytoplankton) come in a remarkable number of forms. If they swim at all, they cannot swim very fast (figure 3.1). They rely on the tides and currents to propel them through the water, creating a nutritious soup for filter-feeding animals such as oysters, scallops, sea cucumbers, shrimp, worms, and myriad other creatures that capture plankton as they float by. Plankton dazzle the imagination by their sheer numbers and variety and their great importance as a food

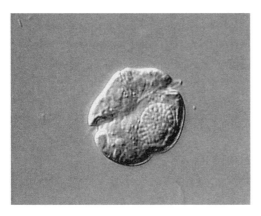

Figure 3.1. Many kinds of phytoplankton (microscopic plants) occur in Florida waters, including this dinoflagellate alga (*Karenia brevis*), shown here highly magnified. (Copyrighted material used with permission from Bigelow Laboratory for Ocean Sciences.)

source. Most fish and invertebrates start life as planktonic larvae. Plankton can even appear magical when luminescent forms sparkle brightly as swimmers pass through them at night.

Bacteria Rule

And what about bacteria? Most of us have never seen bacteria and may associate them solely with infectious diseases. But bacteria, although tiny, play critical roles in curing disease and maintaining animal health, ecosystems, and even the air we breathe. They were living on earth long before plants and animals and have always dominated life on our planet. Bacteria support entire food webs. Some photosynthesize; others break down dead plants and animals and transform inorganic materials into organic compounds, making food available to other organisms. Bacteria also become food themselves.

Algae: Salad of the Estuary

Algae may seem like something green with an annoying habit of growing on your outdoor deck. But algae come in many colors, shapes, and sizes, from tiny, single-celled organisms to the large seaweeds common along our coasts (plate 4). Single-celled algae are abundant in the estuary and are an important food for animals such as fiddler crabs and snails. Algae appear in many settings. Some live in the mud and sand, while others drift about in the water or grow attached to oysters, crabs, and other estuarine inhabitants. All are food sources, and some provide shelter. Algae also help us to understand estuarine dynamics. When too many nutrients flood off the land and pollute the waters, algal blooms may indicate that something is awry, especially when the blooms are large, frequent, or persistent.

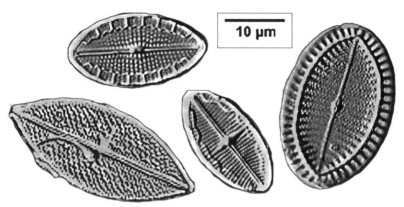

Figure 3.2. Diatoms are tiny single-celled algae that live in silica shells. These diatoms are highly magnified. (Photos courtesy of Jacqueline Huvane and Duke University Wetland Center.)

Diatoms: Algae That Live in Glass Houses

We can't forget to mention diatoms. These beautiful single-celled microorganisms are algae, some golden or reddish-brown and others brilliant green, that live in glassy silica shells (figure 3.2). Diatoms account for about one-fourth of all plant and plant-like life on earth by weight. They always reside in water and provide high-quality nutrition to numerous animals, from plankton to whales. Some glide slowly along slime that they produce, and others don't move at all. Their nourishment comes from photosynthesis or from the organic compounds produced by bacteria. Diatoms are a plentiful food source for many estuarine animals. Fiddler crabs pick them out of the mud, clams siphon them from the water, fish grab them as the mud is disturbed, and sea cucumbers grasp them with tentacles. We use their empty shells, mined from geological deposits of diatomaceous earth, for products like pool filters and scouring agents. Diatoms also produce at least one-fourth of the air we breathe.

Small Things That Make a Difference

These organisms are just a few of the multitudes that make up the estuarine system. To the uninitiated, hearing their names sounds like a foreign language—bryozoans, amphipods, nudibranchs, polychaetes, tunicates, and many others that may seem strange. The Calusa probably knew about most of them and surely enjoyed watching them and musing about their behavior and interactions. Learning about a few helps us to discover aspects of the estuary that we might not normally contemplate. The entire web of life forms a wonderful and complex brocade: changing one part of the fabric always affects many others.

4

ᬛᬛᬛᬛᬛᬛ

Mudflats

What You Don't See Is What You Get

Mudflats are open intertidal areas with almost no rooted plants (figure 4.1). Most Calusa villages had mudflats in their front yards. At first glance, you might think that nothing much ever happens there. But mudflats are far from lifeless. They support a vigorous community of algae, fungi, bacteria, and an assortment of animals that spend most or all of their time there. The life forms and activities in mudflats generate sustenance for the estuary, producing foods and compounds that support other organisms.

Mudflats support life through *photosynthesis*—a chemical reaction that converts water and carbon dioxide into sugars, starches, and cellulose. We usually associate photosynthesis with green leafy plants. But where does photosynthesis happen in a mudflat? It all takes place in the top tenth of an inch or so of the mud, in the cells of tiny single-celled organisms—blue-green algae, diatoms, and others. In this thin layer, enough light is received to allow photosynthesis. But below the thin upper layer is a much thicker zone where oxygen is scarce. There is life here, too, but only for organisms that can burrow or those that can survive without oxygen (called *anaerobes*).

The Calusa watched changes in the mudflats every day. If you were to observe a mudflat for twenty-four hours, you would see a procession of organisms going into and coming out of the mud in response to the tides. Permanent residents include burrowers such as marine worms, clams, crabs, and amphipods (small crustaceans with several pairs of legs). Some of these animals filter their food from the water above. Others eat the mud itself, finding nutrition in the many tiny animals, plants, bacteria, animal feces, and organic compounds within it. Still others are voracious predators that gobble down fellow mudflat residents.

When tides cover the mudflat with water each day, the organisms respond. Surface-dwelling snails graze on the thin layer of algae that covers the mud, while filter-feeding invertebrates such as clams filter the tidal water to sieve out bits of food. As the tide recedes, fiddler crabs emerge from their burrows, and shore birds take fish, snails, shrimp, and crabs.

Figure 4.1. A mudflat at low tide. (Photo by Stacey Breheny.)

Mudflats are distinctly underappreciated. Alas, some people consider them useless real estate. But mudflats support communities of animals that are important to people, such as fish and shellfish.

On a broader scale, mudflats help sustain all life and are major players in global climate conditions. How? You may smell the answer as you walk through the mud—sulfur compounds, reminiscent of the smell of rotten eggs. As countless bacteria work silently to break down organic matter, they produce sulfur compounds that are released into the water and the air. Sulfur is a vital building block for all life. We couldn't survive without sulfur in our systems—nor could any other life on the planet. In the air, sulfur helps to balance atmospheric chemistry. It also helps rain to form as water condenses on sulfate particles. In short: sulfur is great stuff, and bacteria unlock it from decaying matter and allow it to be recycled back into the biosphere (figure 4.2). Mudflats are huge players in this global recycling system.

The Calusa knew mudflats and their residents well. Most of us know little about mud dwellers because they live in the mud and are hard to see. But there is plenty to discover. In addition to tiny microorganisms, worms, and clams, which are most abundant, others also burrow in or cruise the mud surface. Let's take a look at a few of these characters.

The Calusa and Their Legacy

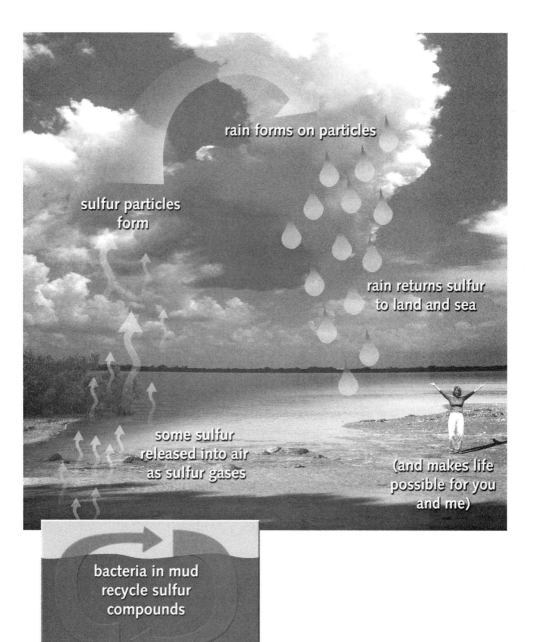

rain forms on particles

sulfur particles form

rain returns sulfur to land and sea

some sulfur released into air as sulfur gases

(and makes life possible for you and me)

bacteria in mud recycle sulfur compounds

Figure 4.2. The sulfur cycle. (Graphic by Dale Johnson.)

Fiddler Crabs: A Mudflat Favorite

At low tide, herds of common fiddler crabs (*Uca* spp.) emerge from the mud to feed (plate 5). Fiddlers are one of the most abundant salt marsh animals and certainly one of the most fascinating to watch. The male crabs have one claw much larger than the other, sometimes accounting for half the crab's body weight. They use it to attract female crabs but can't eat with it. When not grazing on the remains of dead animals and plants or on algae, fiddlers live in burrows up to three feet deep, finding protection against predators and temperature extremes. The burrows are deeper than the water table so that water, critical to fiddler crab survival, is available even at low tide. When above ground, fiddlers must carry water in their gill chambers to enable respiration, to help sort food particles, and to keep themselves cool. At high tide, some fiddlers plug their burrows with mud to keep lurking predators out. Fiddler crabs are a favorite food of larger crabs, fish, birds, and raccoons that visit the mudflat during low tide. Fisherfolk report that fiddlers make good bait, and scientists use the crabs in biological research.

Horseshoe Crabs: An Ancient Parade

Each spring ushers in an ancient migration. Thousands of horseshoe crabs (*Limulus polyphemus*) emerge from the mud of deep winter waters and head for shore to mate and lay eggs. Horseshoe crabs are closely related to spiders and have been on earth for over 200 million years. Today horseshoe crabs cover springtime beaches at high tide. The females burrow in the sand to lay hundreds of green eggs. Within an hour or two they depart into the water with the falling tide. Horseshoe crabs, with their armored exoskeletons and pointed tails, may look formidable and are often spurned by people (figure 4.3). But they are actually harmless—their mouths cannot bite, their claws do not pinch, and their tails merely help them balance, burrow, and turn upright after tumbling in the waves. Horseshoe crabs are directly useful to people in medical and biological research. They are also threatened by over-harvesting for use as conch and eel bait.

Tiny Crustaceans: Amphipods, Isopods, Copepods, and Ostracods

Turn over a shovel-full of mud and you will see hundreds of tiny multilegged crustaceans hopping and wiggling. These small, primitive crustaceans include amphipods, isopods, copepods (figure 4.4), and ostracods. Dozens of

Figure 4.3. A horseshoe crab (*Limulus polyphemus*) among shallow sea grasses. (Photo by Tammy Johnson.)

species live in the estuary, in practically every imaginable habitat—in the mud, among oysters, in the sea grass substrates, in the water column, crawling over algae and hydroid masses, and attached to numerous animals as parasites. Most beachcombers have witnessed the large amphipods called beach hoppers or beach fleas (*Orchestia* spp.) jumping from seaweed washed ashore. All of these numerous crustaceans are an essential food source for fish, crabs, birds, and many other creatures. Although the crustaceans are enormously abundant in healthy habitats, environmental challenges such as pollution and dredging can completely eliminate them.

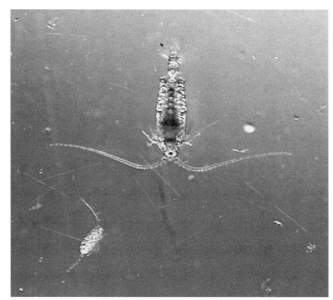

Figure 4.4. This copepod (*Calanus* sp.), seen here through the lens of a microscope, occurs throughout the world's oceans. (Copyrighted material used with permission from Bigelow Laboratory for Ocean Sciences.)

Worms That Live in Tubes: The Polychaetes

You have to get your feet muddy to investigate tube-dwelling polychaete worms. Not all polychaetes live in tubes, but many do. Polychaetes are segmented worms with bristles down their sides, ranging from tiny worms a fraction of an inch long to some over several feet long. They all live in marine habitats. Mud-dwelling tubeworms build U-shaped tubes out of mucous and sand or mud. If you look carefully, you may see tubes of the decorator worm (*Diopatra cuprea*), with its embedded bits of shell and seaweed (plate 6), or of the stickworm (*Owenia fusiformis*), with its overlapping roof-tile sand grains. You may also notice the hollow white-tipped tubes of the parchment worm (*Chaetopterus variopedatus*) or the tentacles of the medusa worm (*Loimia medusa*) sticking out of the mud or even hear the creaking sound made by the green tube worm (*Loimia viridis*). Some polychaetes filter feed with feathery tentacles or pass water through the tube across modified gills. Others pop out of the tube to capture prey or trap plankton on mucous-covered protrusions that then move the food into their mouth. These many and varied worms are favored foods for fish, waterbirds, and numerous other members of the food web. Their huge New England relatives are so plump and tasty that they are kings of the commercial bait empire. Some Gulf coast fisherfolk use polychaetes too, digging out their burrows at low tide.

Mud Brittle Stars

Buried up to five inches in fine mud lives a gangly sea star with a small central disk and long fragile arms. The mud brittle star (*Ophionephthys limicola*) sticks the tips of its long snake-like arms above the mud to collect nutritious decaying plant material, passing the food down to its mouth by using the tube feet along its arms. Five triangular jaws with central columns of teeth direct the food into a simple digestive system; after processing in the stomach, any undigested remains squirt back out the mouth. A brittle star's delicate arms break easily, but this is not a big ordeal—the arms contain no vital organs and regenerate easily and quickly. Brittle stars begin life as planktonic larvae, floating near the water surface, and later sink down to the floor as mini-adults. Although well hidden when in the mud, the stars become an easy target for hungry fish when they are caught writhing across the muddy bottom. A buried mud brittle star is hard to spot, but you may see other brittle stars on the mud (*Ophiolepus elegans*) (plate 7) or crawling on sponges and sea grass blades (*Ophioderma brevispinum* and *Ophiothrix angulata*).

Sturdy Clams: The Quahogs

The heavy-shelled quahog clam (*Mercenaria campechiensis*) buries itself an inch or two into the mud. It uses its large soft foot to dig down and anchor itself. To feed and breathe, the clam extends a siphon tube up through the mud and draws in water rich in oxygen and food. Quahogs are fast growers that can weigh up to five pounds (figure 4.5) and commonly live for about twenty-five years. Crabs, whelks, and stingrays love to dine on quahogs, and many animals favor the empty clam shells as good hiding spots. The Calusa also enjoyed dining on these large mollusks. They used the shells for tools such as anvils and chopping blades and (along with other food refuse) as material for building mounds. To find out more about the Calusa, scientists look at the growth rings in quahog shells to study the seasons when people lived in different places and at the geochemical composition of the shells to study ancient water temperatures and climate changes. Quahogs continue to be important to Floridians. Today we raise and harvest quahogs commercially (*Mercenaria mercenaria*) and savor steamed or raw clams, spaghetti with clam sauce, and clam chowder.

Figure 4.5. A quahog clam (*Mercenaria campechiensis*) collected from a shelly mudflat. (Photo by Karen Walker.)

Ever Dined at an Oyster Bar?

On the surface of the mud but below mean tide lives the common oyster (*Crassostrea virginica*). Oysters anchor themselves to foundations such as rocks, shells, mangrove roots, or dock pilings and clump into communities known as oyster bars or reefs (plate 8). Oysters make a living by filtering tiny plankton from the water. Filtering rates can be staggering; as enormous amounts of water pass through the oyster's system, it helps to cleanse the water in the estuary. In turn, oyster feces enrich the bottom sediments and become food for plants and other animals in the food web. The oyster bar serves as an anchorage for mussels, barnacles, and other invertebrates. This community also provides habitat for a wide variety of snails, crabs, shrimp, and fish, while stabilizing the muddy bottom and protecting the coast from storm damage. Oysters make a good meal for cruising crown conchs, stone crabs, and foraging birds.

Like today's people, the Calusa relished a meal of Florida oysters. Massive amounts of oyster shells make up some Calusa mounds and other earthworks (figure 4.6). The earthworks at villages near oyster bars were almost entirely made of oyster shells. Scientists also learn about environmental changes during the time of the Calusa by looking carefully at oyster shells from Calusa sites for signs of small mollusks and sponges that indicate changes in water salinity and thus mark environmental changes.

The Crown Conch: King of the Mud

The mighty little crown conch (*Melongena corona*), named for its crown-like shell, is a snail and thus a member of the enormous and varied phylum Mollusca (mollusks), along with clams and even octopus and squid. Conchs and other snails move around on a soft, flat foot that secretes slime to help them glide (plate 9). When temperatures drop, the crown conch may bury itself in mud to stay warm. A keen sense of smell leads conchs to dead animals, their typical meal, but crown conchs may also dine on live oysters and snails. To eat, they use their foot to clasp onto the mollusk and stick a long, toothy "radula" or tongue into the shells, scraping out soft tissues into their mouths. When crown conchs die, their shells provide a roomy apartment for house-hunting hermit crabs.

The Calusa ate crown conchs and used their shells for tools such as hammers. Discarded shells became part of the building material used for earthworks. Modern oyster fishers once worried that conchs could harm their business, but scientists have learned that crown conchs do not deplete oyster populations.

What Is an Invertebrate?

Invertebrates are animals without backbones or spinal columns. The estuary is full of invertebrates, including shrimp, jellyfish, worms, anemones, and oysters. Invertebrates are critical players in the estuarine ecosystem.

ᗏᗏᗏᗏᗏᗏ

Figure 4.6. Remnant of midden made of fish bones, charcoal, dirt, and many oyster shells. (The stick shows height in meters.) (Photo by William Marquardt.)

Mudflats: What You Don't See Is What You Get　　　23

A Study in Pink: The Roseate Spoonbill

You may think you've seen a flamingo, but look again. The roseate spoonbill (*Ajaia ajaja*), with its bright pink feathers and odd spoon-shaped bill, is more striking in appearance than most other mudflat visitors (plate 10). Spoonbills nest in the mangrove treetops and hang out in shallow near-shore waters, wandering through the mud and swinging their spoon-shaped beaks from side to side through the water. The beak is loaded with nerve endings that sense when it hits food—small crustaceans, mollusks, insects, and fish. A diet heavy in shrimp and other colorful morsels helps to make the feathers pink, because the birds cannot produce the red pigment themselves.

Archaeological remains suggest that the Calusa did not often eat wading birds, though their likeness is found in some Calusa art. In the 1800s and early 1900s spoonbills and many large wading birds became rare during a craze in American hunting. Thanks to state and federal regulations, these birds are now protected and continue to delight viewers with their magnificent pink presence in today's south Florida estuaries.

5

᪥᪥᪥᪥᪥᪥

Sea Grass Beds

Just beyond the mudflat, in slightly deeper water, lies another amazing and dynamic place—the sea grass beds (figure 5.1). These grassy flats were extremely important to the Calusa because so many of the animals they harvested for food lived, ate, or found protection among the grasses.

Sea grasses live underwater in shallow coastal areas in many parts of the world. The leaves of some species (but not all) are narrow and resemble grass blades—hence the name; but in fact they are not grasses at all. They are flowering plants that live under water. There are over fifty kinds of sea grasses around the world, seven of which live along Florida's coasts. Florida Bay and the Charlotte Harbor/Pine Island Sound estuaries have the greatest acreage of sea grass meadows in south Florida.

Sea grass beds are one of Florida's most productive environments. They are important to us in numerous ways:

- Sea grass meadows provide hiding places for both predators and prey and serve as critical nurseries for fish and shellfish.
- The plants provide oxygen needed by fish and absorb carbon dioxide released by fish as part of their respiration process.
- Huge numbers of tiny organisms live on sea grass leaves. These organisms and the sea grass leaves provide food for many marine animals, including sea turtles and manatees.
- Sea grasses help stabilize shorelines by baffling waves and can even alter the flow of currents.
- Sea grass roots and rhizomes keep the sea bottom stable.
- Sea grasses maintain water clarity by trapping fine particles with their leaves and by removing nutrients from the water that might otherwise cause blooms of algae that cloud the water or cause toxic red tides.
- Sea grasses convert nutrients from the water into food that other organisms can use.
- Dead sea grasses wash up into shoreline areas and become food for many organisms in areas where food may be scarce (figure 5.2).

Figure 5.1. Underwater view of healthy sea grass bed. (Photo by Heather Dine, courtesy of Florida Keys National Marine Sanctuary.)

Perhaps the most important function of sea grass meadows is their role as vital spawning sites and nurseries for some of Florida's most valued marine creatures, including many that the Calusa ate and that we eat today. They use the sea grasses for protection and feeding of their offspring. In fact, more than 70 percent of Florida's commercially harvested fish and invertebrates (including crabs, lobsters, and shrimp) live among sea grasses when young.

Figure 5.2. Dead sea grasses provide food for detritus scavengers. (Photo by Darcie Mac-Mahon.)

ᘓᘓᘓᘓᘓᘓ

Sea Grasses and Light

Sea grasses are flowering plants and require sunlight to survive. Through the process of photosynthesis, sunlight provides the energy for all plants to manufacture food. Sea grasses grow in shallow water where sunlight can penetrate to the sea bottom. In today's estuaries, human-caused pollution and siltation from dredging and filling can cloud the water and kill sea grasses, destroying the entire sea grass community.

ᘓᘓᘓᘓᘓᘓ

Sea grasses are also good hosts. If you look closely, the surface of a sea grass blade looks like a veritable zoo, covered with other plants and animals (plate 11). More than one hundred species of algae live on the sea grass blades. Some of the single-celled diatom algae secrete slimy tracks along which they move over the grass blades; others anchor themselves and do not move at all. Animals also take up residence on the sea grass blades, including bryozoans, hydroids, tube worms, and barnacles. Residents of the grass blades are important members of the marine food web and support other species that humans eat.

Less permanent visitors come to find food in the sea grass beds. Grazing sea slugs and snails, sea urchins, brittle stars, and fish eat the tiny plants and animals that live on the sea grass blades. Manatees and sea turtles eat the grass blades and the algae growing on and among them. Wading birds, eagles, ospreys, and migrating coastal birds forage in the grasses for fish and invertebrates.

All this oozing, grazing, and chomping activity produces an assortment of by-products. Like thousands of crumbs from thousands of dinner plates, particles of organic matter drift down to the sea bottom. And like a rich garden soil, the sediments under the sea grasses harbor hundreds of species of invertebrate animals. In one square meter of estuarine bottom, you can find thousands of marine worms, amphipods, and hosts of other invertebrates. Some of these animals live out their entire lives within the sediments. Others stay there for a period and then emerge when conditions are right for feeding or reproduction. Even after sea grasses die, they wash ashore and decay, becoming food for myriad creatures.

The animals that depend on sea grass beds include many Calusa and contemporary favorites—bay scallops, hard clams, spiny lobsters, stone crabs, pink shrimp, lightning whelks, pear whelks, horse conchs, grouper, snapper, redfish, seatrout, mullet, pinfish, pompano, needle fish, sea turtles, and manatees. Clearly, we must preserve sea grasses to preserve healthy estuaries and our seafood supply.

Like mudflats, sea grass meadows are dynamic places. Moving among the sea grasses, on and above the sea bottom, are crabs, shrimp, sea stars, and numerous mollusks and fish. They feed on the residents attached to sea grasses and reproduce in the meadows. Let's take a glimpse at some sea grass denizens.

Diners' Delights: Stone Crabs and Blue Crabs

Among the dozens of crab species that live among the sea grasses, two appear prominently on most seafood menus today and were also favorites of the Calusa—stone crabs (*Menippe mercenaria*) and blue crabs (*Callinectes sapidus*) (figure 5.3). Stone crabs live mainly along Florida's southwest coast. Blues, which once occurred only across the western Atlantic and Gulf of Mexico, have now spread to many locations worldwide where they are commercially harvested. Both burrow into the soft sands of the sea grass meadows and emerge with the arrival of high tide to feed. These crabs are *omnivores* and will eat just about anything, recycling dead matter and detritus as well as choosing live meals. As *predators*, stone crabs use their powerful claws to crush oysters and clams or chip away at their edges until they can access the meat. Large blue crabs do the same. Stone crabs may be stronger, but blues are excellent swimmers by virtue of their paddle-like rear legs. Both crabs provide secondary services to their community. Barnacles and other invertebrates anchor onto older crab shells. Stone crab burrows provide shelter and protection for other crabs, shrimp, worms, and some fish. And plenty of estuarine residents enjoy crabs for dinner—sea turtles, sharks, fish, rays, and birds.

The human taste for crabs is centuries old and led to a booming fishing industry in the twentieth century. Restrictions now regulate U.S. crab harvests to protect the populations. People harvest the whole blue crab but take only the stone crab's claws. The stone crab will generate new claws within a year if it manages to survive, which is a challenge, because it uses its claws for both feeding and defense.

Shrimp among the Sea Grasses

The word "shrimp" brings to mind plates of steaming seafood and cocktail sauce. In fact, the United States is one of the world's largest consumers of shrimp, and Florida's Gulf coast boasts huge harvests of Penaid shrimp, a

a

b

Figure 5.3. Florida's best-known crabs: (a) blue crab (*Callinectes sapidus*). (Photo by Ken Scudder, courtesy of Sylvia Scudder.) (b) stone crab (*Menippe mercenaria*). (Photo by Jeff Gage.)

group that includes the valuable pink (*Farfantepenaeus duorarum*), white (*Litopenaeus setiferus*), and brown (*Farfantepenaeus aztecus*) shrimp (plate 12). It is likely that the Calusa ate shrimp, although their remains do not preserve well in archaeological deposits. Tiny shrimp jaws from a well-preserved site on coastal Georgia confirm that Indian people living near those estuaries enjoyed shrimp. The Calusa were a net-fishing society in an estuary teeming with shrimp. It is almost certain that their nets brought up shrimp—and a good guess that they ate them.

All commercially harvested shrimp along the Gulf rely on the estuary early in life. Adults spawn far offshore, and the new larvae wash into estuaries with the tides and find protection and food amid the grass beds. Pink and brown shrimp burrow in the mud by day and emerge at night to feed, while white shrimp burrow by night and emerge during the day. Molting as they grow, the shrimp mature within a few months and return to deeper waters. All are esteemed foods for many marine creatures, including sharks, skates and rays, most fish, and sea turtles.

Figure 5.4. The large claw of the snapping shrimp (*Alpheus hetero-chaelis*) makes a loud snapping sound. (Photo by Jeff Gage.)

Sea grass meadows are also home to several smaller, noncommercial shrimp. Grass shrimp (*Palaemonetes* spp.) live by the millions in the shallow meadows and feast upon diatoms and microorganisms in the mud. The green arrow shrimp (*Tozeuma carolinense*) and broken-backed shrimp (*Hippolyte zostericola*) are well disguised among the green grass blades. Distinctively crooked with L-shaped backs, these shrimps graze on the algae and invertebrates attached to the grass blades. The secretive snapping shrimp (*Alpheus heterochaelis*) hides under debris or on oyster reefs and is often heard before it is seen (figure 5.4). This shrimp makes a loud popping sound when it snaps its claw shut, thereby stunning the small fish and invertebrates it feeds upon and perhaps serving as a sexual and defensive device. Any snorkeler knows the sound of snapping shrimp, whose loud pops may even be heard above water.

Lightning Whelks: Magnificent Snails

The stately lightning whelk (*Busycon sinistrum*) glides over the surface of the sea grass beds and hunts for tasty sand-dwelling bivalves (figure 5.5). This large *gastropod* (literally meaning a "belly-footed" mollusk) feeds almost exclusively on bivalves. The whelk extends its ample black foot down into the sand to grasp a clam, forces open the shells with the lip of its shell, and scrapes out the flesh with a long ribbon of teeth, or *radula*. In the spring and summer months, female whelks lay their eggs in a long strand of horny disks (figure 5.6). Over the next two months, the eggs mature into tiny whelks

Figure 5.5. A lightning whelk (*Busycon sinistrum*) cruises along the sand on its black foot. (Photo by Robert Repenning, courtesy of Florida Department of Environmental Protection.)

Figure 5.6. A lightning whelk egg case rests on the sand amid sea grasses. (Photo by Robert Repenning, courtesy of Florida Department of Environmental Protection.)

before they hatch from the egg case and begin life in the sea grass beds. If the young snail can avoid becoming dinner for hungry fish, the adult may attain the honorable length of sixteen inches.

Whelks of the genus *Busycon* have lived along eastern American coasts for over 60 million years. Early inhabitants of coastal Florida, including the Calusa, valued whelk meat and used the shells for woodworking tools, hammers, fishing sinkers, net-making tools, drinking vessels, beads, and other personal ornaments. The whelk tool and ornament industry was huge, with shells traded from Florida as far as the Great Lakes and present-day Oklahoma. Various Calusa-made whelk tools and ornaments are featured later in this book.

Old Blue Eyes: The Bay Scallop

As any scalloper can tell you, the tasty bay scallop (*Argopecten irradians*) likes to hang out in sea grass beds. Tiny blue eyes along the edge of the animal's mantle peer out from the crenulated shell (plate 13). When shadows pass by, these light-sensitive eyes trigger the shells to snap shut to avoid danger. The shells also snap shut to propel the scallop through the sea grass beds, forcing out water and moving the animal in short spurts above the sand. Like nearly all bivalves, scallops are filter feeders and pump water through their bodies to filter out plankton.

The Calusa ate plenty of scallops, mostly during the late spring and summer months when big, plump scallops congregate in the grass beds. Archaeologists find scallop shells at most Calusa sites, sometimes in pockets of numerous shells that suggest scallop feasts. Today Florida seafood lovers eat only the round white muscle that holds the bivalve closed. But scallop lovers beware—scallops are sensitive to pollution and coastal dredge and fill operations. Protection of sea grass meadows ensures that scallops will continue to grace our tables.

Mollusks without Shells

South Florida sea grasses are home to a variety of soft-bodied mollusks that have no external shells. Some are nudibranchs (meaning "naked gills"), including the fascinating sea slugs. Their external gills absorb oxygen and pass out wastes. Unique tentacle-like horns allow nudibranchs to smell, and primitive eyes sense gradations in light. In south Florida sea grasses, the rough-backed dorris (*Onchidoris verrucosa*) is a one-inch orange "slug" ornamented with large round tubercles and small brown spots. Look for them among the grasses or on red mangrove roots or pilings.

Sea hares are also mollusks without external shells (they do have a vestigial shell inside their bodies). Although they are seemingly defenseless without shells, some squirt purple ink to distract predators, and some secrete a distasteful ooze. In south Florida, the four-inch ragged sea hare (*Bursatella leachii pleii*) is covered with long fleshy protuberances. This "ragged" look and a green-gray color with dark spots camouflage the hare among the algae it eats. You may also see the spotted sea hare (*Aplysia dactylomela*), with its soft, wide foot.

The lovely lettuce sea slug (*Elysia crispata*) is yet another shell-less mollusk in south Florida waters. Its green ruffled appearance allows it to masquerade perfectly among marine algae (plate 14).

Stars of the Sea Grass Beds

Sea stars, often called starfish, are invertebrates related to sea urchins and sea cucumbers and belong to the "spiny-skinned" phylum Echinodermata. Several live among south Florida sea grasses. Most sea stars feed on other invertebrates, such as urchins, bivalves, and crabs. Suction cups on the sea star's arms capture the prey and can help pull apart bivalves or manipulate snails. The sea star may then extrude part of its stomach through its mouth and insert the stomach into its prey. The stomach releases enzymes that digest the prey's tissues and turn the meal into a hearty soup as the sea star retracts the stomach back inside. Sea stars are very flexible: they use their arm muscles and tube feet to move in any direction and to turn themselves right-side-up.

In south Florida juvenile brown spiny sea stars (*Echinaster spinulosus*) are abundant in the sea grass beds but later move to the muddy bottoms of mangrove channels (plate 15). The large nine-armed sea star (*Luidia senegalensis*) sports more arms than its common five-armed relatives and lives on or under the grass bed sands, feeding on detritus.

What Is a Sand Dollar, Really?

Sand dollars (*Mellita quinquiesperforata*, also called keyhole urchins) are not the storied currency of mermaids but rather are flat sea urchins with very short spines (plate 16). Beachcombers find their bleached white skeletons; but when the urchins are alive, they are covered with a skin of tiny spines that help them move and gather food. The sand dollar's thin, sharp profile allows it to burrow quickly in shallow sand, where it slowly moves along grazing on detritus and diatoms. The "keyholes" in its body let water pass through and prevent waves from lifting the sand dollar and carrying it to shore.

Cucumbers with Feet

Sea cucumbers may resemble a cucumber in shape, but they are really elongated relatives of urchins and sea stars. Tiny tube feet slowly move them a few yards each day. On the cucumber's front end, feathery tentacles surround a mouth and sweep in sand and mud from which the animal digests detritus.

Figure 5.7. A pygmy sea cucumber (*Pentacta pygmaea*). (Photo by Tammy Johnson.)

At the back end is the cucumber's multi-talented anus, which not only expels the animal's sandy feces but also enables respiration as it sucks water into channels that carry oxygen into the lumpy body. Sea cucumbers use their anus in self-defense too, ejecting part of their intestines to distract hungry predators: while they are gobbling the intestines, the cucumber crawls away and regenerates new intestines. Among south Florida sea grasses, you may find the four-inch brown pygmy sea cucumber (*Pentacta pygmaea*) in the grass beds, using its tentacles to sweep the water for food (figure 5.7).

The worm-like white synapta (*Leptosynapta tenuis*), harder to see, lives in U-shaped burrows. We don't know if the Calusa ate sea cucumbers, but some species are prized as food in Asia today.

At Home on a Sea Grass Blade

So many plants and animals take up residence on sea grass blades that it is hard to do them justice (plate 17). Grab a blade and look closely. You will see green algae too numerous to name. You may also see small, round white encrustations, which are the calcium-rich tubes of minute annelid worms. Other less recognizable piggy-backers include primitive animals that live in colonies and feed on nutrients in the surrounding water. Hydroids (*Obelia dichotoma*) are related to the Portuguese man-of-war jellyfish and sport stinging cells on the bushy tufts at the tips of branching stems. Star-like groups of flat sea squirts, the variable encrusting tunicates (*Botryllus planus*), contain many individual orange, purple, yellow, or green animals. Bryozoans (literally, "moss animals") live in branching colonies that look like algae. Under a microscope, you could see many species of diatoms on a grass blade surface. These are just a few of the interesting sidekicks on sea grass, most of which also decorate red mangrove roots and dock pilings. They help to keep the water clear and also serve as food for myriad grazing fish.

Sponges Alive!

We may think of sponges as soft and good for scrubbing, but living sponges are tough and are home to thousands of tiny animals. Originally thought to be plants, these ancient animals bridge the evolutionary gap between single-celled organisms (*protists*) and the more complex jellyfish. Their hair-like flagella beat water through the colony, and special cells trap bacteria and plankton. Some have tough outer skins that contain microscopic needle-like "spicules" that give the sponge a rigid form and can hurt if you try to squeeze one. These gardens of color and form delight many a snorkeler; although more famous in coral reef habitats, sponges also grow in the sea grass meadows. There you may see them between the grass blades, attached to shells or rocks in the sand, or growing directly on the grass blades.

The small but lovely eroded sponge (*Haliclona loosanoffi*) has purple finger-like projections and ranges in size from only one-twentieth of an inch to about three inches (plate 18). The garlic sponge (*Lissodendoryx isodictyalis*), green-gray or tan and amorphous in shape, emits a strong odor of garlic when broken and may fully encompass a sea grass blade. All sponges provide excellent hiding places for many invertebrates and small fish; and some animals, such as the hawksbill sea turtle, love to eat these crunchy colonies.

We don't know if the Calusa used sponges, but today's scientists do study them to learn about aspects of the Calusa environment. Boring sponges (*Cliona* sp.) are so named because they bore tiny holes into the shells of oysters and other shellfish. These holes show up on the shells in Calusa middens and reveal environmental stories. How? Boring sponges prosper in high-salinity water. If midden oysters have sponge holes, the Calusa harvested them from high-salinity waters. If oysters from the same location vary over the years from having holes to not having holes, scientists can tell that the water salinity changed over time. They thus learn about the nature of the nearby waters, which in turn can indicate other environmental changes.

Sea Whips: Animal Apartments That Look Like Plants

The colorful sea whip (*Leptogorgia virgulata*) looks at first glance like a yellow, orange, red, or purple plant (plate 19). But its sturdy outer casing of proteins and calcium is occupied by colonies of animals related to jellyfish and coral. When feeding, the white animals or *polyps* extend out from their own tiny cups in the colorful outer shell. They wave their tentacles to capture floating plankton as cells with stingers called *nematocysts* stun the prey. Sea whips attach themselves to shells and rocks; after storms they may be washed onto the beach still clinging to their anchor. Sea whips can also be host to other animals, including rubber bryozoans (*Alcyonidium hauffi*), another colonial animal that inhabits a gray rubbery skeleton. The bryozoan attaches itself to the sea whip and, like the whip, filters the water for food.

6

૭૭૭૭૭૭

The Sea

Water is the highway of the estuary. All sorts of things travel by water and are moved by the tides, ranging from the salt itself and other nutrients to microscopic organisms, to jellyfish, to large animals such as manatees, sharks, and sea turtles (figure 6.1). Water movement distributes nutrients to new locations and removes wastes. Water connects the estuarine zones and thus facilitates many interactions. In short, water allows things to happen.

On a more global scale, the water in estuaries and oceans plays a big role. More than 70 percent of the earth's surface is covered with water. Fresh water makes up just 3 percent of that, and the rest is held in the oceans. Water recycles over and over between the earth and the atmosphere, evaporating into the air and returning to earth as rain and snow. This cycling of water supports most of the life on earth, including ours.

Did the Calusa value the water of the sea as well as the organisms that live there? Surely they did. Water was their main means of travel, from fishing expeditions to trade and communication to attacks on their enemies. And don't you suppose they enjoyed a swim in the Gulf's blue-green waters?

Passengers on the watery estuarine highway, like the creatures of the mudflats and sea grass beds, are too numerous to mention comprehensively. Let's delve into a few life stories.

Jellyfish: Really Big Plankton

In spite of their size, jellyfish are technically plankton because they depend on currents to get from place to place. Gentle contraction of their bells provides some locomotion, but jellyfish mostly drift with the tides and currents. After a strong offshore wind, the estuary can be full of jellies. True jellyfish, like their relatives the corals, anemones, and hydroids, have stinging cells used to stun prey. Some pack a punch worse than others. Along the southern Gulf coast, the common moon jelly (*Aurelia aurita*) is more beautiful than troublesome, with short tentacles ringing the clear or bluish bell. The up-

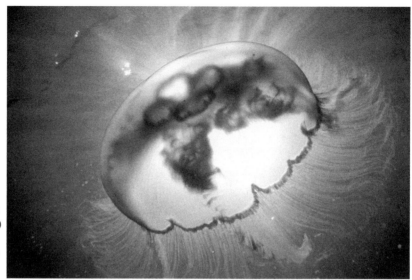

Figure 6.1. A moon jelly (*Aurelia aurita*) drifts with the water currents. (Photo by Anne DuPont.)

side-down jellyfish (*Cassiopeia xamachana*) floats like others with its bell up, but it rests on the estuary bottom upside-down to sun its lacy arms (plate 20). These arms are home to algae that (through photosynthesis) provide the jelly with food and oxygen, in turn earning protection from predators by the jelly's sting.

Perhaps most common in estuarine waters is the harmless comb jelly (*Mnemiopsis mccradyi*), which lacks stinging cells and is thus not a true jellyfish at all. This perfectly transparent animal is named for the comb-like rows of cilia that help the animal move, while two short tentacles with sticky cells capture passing plankton. The jelly's combs shimmer iridescently by day and are brightly luminescent at night (plate 21).

Who would eat a jellyfish? Plenty of predators munch on jellyfish, including sea turtles such as the leatherback, which eats almost nothing else yet can weigh more than one ton. We don't know if the Calusa ate jellyfish, since no parts survive in archaeological deposits, but they are popular on Asian menus today.

Squid of Many Colors

The brief thumbstall squid (*Lolliguncula brevis*) swims in schools through estuarine waters (figure 6.2). This ten-inch squid is speckled with purple but can change colors, from clear to black, when startled or to match its environment. Some turn red when in pursuit of prey. Squids also release clouds of "ink" to confuse predators and conceal their retreat. Squids have great vision and use their ten arms to capture small fish and crustaceans. They can swim head-first by using side fins; but when frightened they jet quickly backward by squeezing water from a large internal cavity. Squids are not only fascinating to watch while snorkeling or in aquaria but are also good to eat—calamari, anyone? We can't determine whether the Calusa ate squid, since there is little that could survive the test of time and soils.

A Horse Is a Horse, Unless It's a Seahorse

Seahorses, so-named because their heads look very horse-like, are actually fish—and curious fish indeed. Their curly tails help them hang onto sea grass blades, and tiny fins propel them slowly through the water. Seahorses can change color to match their surroundings. Their tubular snouts quickly suck up small invertebrates and larvae. Perhaps most unusual is that seahorse males become pregnant. A female deposits about 300 eggs in a belly pouch near the male's tail, and eight to ten days later the tiny seahorses emerge. Pipefish (seahorse relatives) have similar snouts, and the males also carry eggs in a pouch. But pipefish bodies are long, straight, and thin, and they swim along the bottom like snakes or rest camouflaged among grass blades (plate 22). In south Florida estuaries, you may discover the lined seahorse (*Hippocampus erectus*) moseying through the grass beds as well as several species of pipefish. Surely the Calusa enjoyed these fascinating animals, and we value them today as aquarium pets.

Flying through Water: The Rays and Skates

The sight is unforgettable—rays and skates flying gracefully through the water undulating their large, wing-like pectoral (side) fins. Such a sighting is practically guaranteed while snorkeling in shallow south Florida waters.

Figure 6.2. Brief thumbstall squid (*Lolliguncula brevis*). (Drawing by Dale Johnson.)

These flat, kite-shaped animals evolved from sharks about 400 million years ago, adopting the flattened shape that makes it easy for them to cruise over sea bottoms in search of mollusks, crustaceans, or worms. All skates and rays, like the sharks, have skeletons made of cartilage instead of bone and boast a tough skin covered with tooth-like scales. Some can bounce electric sonar signals off the sea floor to locate prey.

If you've taken a swim in south Florida waters, chances are you've seen a startled southern stingray (*Dasyatis americana*) rise from the sand and fly away (figure 6.3). Watch your step and shuffle your feet as you go—a stinging barb on the stingray's whip-like tail can inflict a serious wound. Most rays have stingers, but don't worry about the smooth butterfly ray (*Gymnura micrura*), which also rests beneath the sand but lacks a stinging spine. You can also relax around the clearnose skate (*Raja eglanteria*)—none of the skates have spines.

The Calusa valued rays for many reasons. Judging from ample remains in middens, they enjoyed rays as food. They used stingray spines as sharp tools, such as fish gigs or spears and perforators. The Calusa also seem to have used ray vertebrae as beads, and a charming little carved ray-like figure from Key Marco may have been someone's favorite personal ornament (figure 6.4).

Tasty Fishes

The estuary was for the Calusa and is for us today a fisher's paradise. Whether fishing with nets, hook and line, or spear, for commerce or for sport, all Flor-

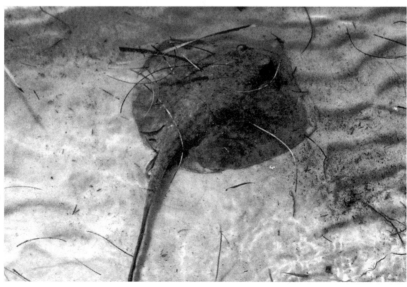

Figure 6.3. A southern stingray (*Dasyatis americana*) cruises close to the mud. (Photo by Ken Scudder.)

The Calusa and Their Legacy

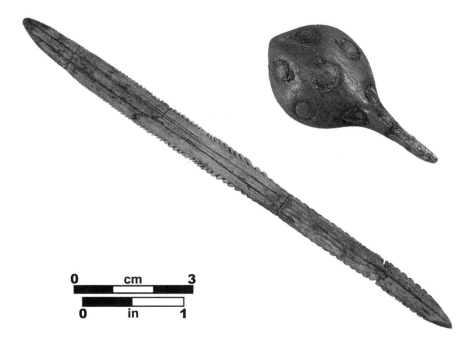

```
0        cm        3
▓▓▓▓▓▓░░░░░▓▓▓▓▓
▓▓▓▓▓▓░░░░░▓▓▓▓▓
0        in        1
```

ida fisherfolk know the estuary. Numerous fish species populate the shallow waters, nurtured by plentiful food resources and protected from deep-water predators. Most of our commercial fish spend their young lives in the estuary.

You might use abundant small estuarine fish as bait, but the Calusa ate them in large quantities, especially pinfish (*Lagodon rhomboides*), pigfish (*Orthopristis chrysoptera*), and hardhead catfish (*Arius felis*). Otherwise our fish dinners resemble those of the Calusa (plate 23):

- The Gulf flounder (*Paralichthys albigutta*) rests under the sand, changing color to match its environment.
- Mullets (*Mugil* sp.) mate offshore in winter, and the young come inshore in summer. They move in schools through the estuary and feed on algae, detritus, and tiny animals in the mud.
- Juvenile redfish (*Sciaenops ocellatus*) cruise the estuary for the first four years of life and then join their elders in deeper water.
- Juvenile mangrove snappers (*Lutjanus griseus*) hang out in the mangrove root shallows.
- Sheepsheads (*Archosargus probatocephalus*) may be nearby, nibbling on barnacles and mollusks.
- Black drums (*Pogonias cromis*) search among oyster bars for mollusks and crustaceans.
- Spotted seatrout (*Cynoscion nebulosus*) rove through the sea grass beds looking for shrimp and small fish.

Figure 6.4. A stingray spine point and wooden carving of a ray or skate. (Photos by Jeff Gage, graphic by Pat Payne.)

- Snooks (*Centropomus undecimalis*) school along mangrove shorelines and passes, feeding on fish and larger crustaceans.
- Not often eaten, but still king of the sportfishing world, the magnificent tarpon (*Megalops atlanticus*) dazzles viewers as it leaps into the air, flashing silver from its enormous body (weighing 40 to 200 pounds).

All of these fish rely on the estuary for food and protection and coexist in a wonderful watery web of life. Think about the big picture next time you fish!

Manatees: Elephants of the Sea

Sirenians (the scientific name of the group that includes manatees) are sea mammals that evolved from land mammals over 60 million years ago and lived in Florida at least 45 million years ago. Today manatees are most closely related to elephants. The West Indian manatee (*Trichechus manatus*) is one of four living Sirenian species worldwide and occurs from the southern United States through the Caribbean and eastern Central and South America in warm shallow coastal waters, rivers, and springs (figure 6.5). In the estuary, these slow-moving mammals graze on sea grasses for about five hours each day. This fibrous, sandy diet soon wears out their teeth, which migrate forward and drop out as new teeth emerge. Manatees can reach more than ten feet in length and weigh over a ton. Although they can swim in short bursts at fifteen miles per hour, they usually travel at about two to six miles per hour and often hang below the water's surface, coming up only to breathe. Surprisingly agile and buoyant in water, a manatee may perform somersaults, barrel rolls, or head and tail stands and glide upside-down. Naturally curious, manatees like to explore. They communicate by sight, touch, smell, and sound, emitting squeals that include sounds that humans can hear. Some migrate long distances to northerly waters in the summer and gather back in warmer climes for winter.

௸௸௸௸௸௸

Did You Know?

A female redfish can bear one trillion eggs. The larvae drift into the estuary, and the young reside there until grown, munching on plankton and finding safety among the sea grass blades and later in the mangrove roots. But there is a lot of death along the way: out of those trillion eggs, one female may survive to adulthood and head out to sea to reproduce.

௸௸௸௸௸௸

Figure 6.5. West Indian manatees (*Trichechus manatus*). (Photo by Patrick M. Rose, courtesy of Save the Manatee Club.)

The West Indian manatee is highly endangered throughout its range. The Calusa may have eaten them, because their bones are present (though scant) in archaeological sites. The Seminoles and Miccosukees occasionally hunted them for meat, as did European and later American settlers. But today most are killed by collisions with boats and barges. About 3,500 survive in Florida waters. Many have had close calls, marked by propeller scars on their backs. Other threats include entanglement in fishing gear and flood-control structures, pollution, poaching and vandalism, and harassment as well as cold weather, red tide, and a naturally low reproductive rate. Perhaps most critical for the manatee's future is the rapid loss of habitat, a loss that affects the future of all estuarine animals.

Sea Turtles: They Get Around

Out of seven species of sea turtles worldwide, five are found in Florida waters: the loggerhead (*Caretta caretta*) (plate 24), green (*Chelonia mydas*), leatherback (*Dermochelys coriacea*), hawksbill (*Eretmochelys imbricata*), and Kemp's ridley (*Lepidochelys kempi*) sea turtles. Four of these are endangered; and the fifth, the loggerhead, is threatened. Sea turtles have roamed warm shallow seas for about 150 million years. They travel huge distances between feeding and nesting grounds, sometimes thousands of miles, and mysteriously revisit the same beach for each nesting cycle. Scientists do not yet understand how they navigate—perhaps by smell or by magnetic tracking. All come ashore to nest and struggle up the beach above the high-tide line to dig shallow holes for their eggs.

The Kemp's ridley nests on only one beach in Mexico, but the others can be found nesting on Florida beaches, especially along the Atlantic. If you are lucky, you may see a sea turtle while swimming or boating. The green sea turtle, the only vegetarian, munches on sea grasses and mangrove leaves. You might also encounter the jellyfish-eating leatherback, the crab-eating Kemp's ridley, or a loggerhead foraging on crabs, jellyfish, sponges, and mollusks. Hawksbills usually hang out near coral reefs and prefer to eat sponges but may also snack on red mangroves.

The Calusa ate sea turtles and used their bones to make tools, such as the gauges that gave fishing nets a uniform mesh size. But their harvest was modest and did not endanger turtles. Today sea turtles face many challenges. Their nesting sites, also prime beach properties, are often altered or destroyed by humans. Natural predators and human activities can ruin a young hatchling's chance of survival. Shrimp nets without "turtle excluding devices" easily drown sea turtles, and plastic garbage (such as plastic bags, which resemble floating jellyfish) can choke them to death. In some places in the world, people still eat sea turtle meat and eggs and make goods from their leather and shells. Fortunately, conservation efforts are on the rise worldwide. You can help by learning more.

Bottlenose Dolphins: The Great Communicators

Swimmers, listen in! Bottlenose dolphins (*Tursiops truncatus*) are the most common marine mammals in south Florida estuaries, and they like to talk. They navigate and hunt for fish by sonar, making clicking sounds that travel through water and identify the size, shape, and location of objects. Dolphins also talk to each other, using a well-developed language of sounds, and communicate with other types of behavior too. In fact, scientists have discovered that dolphins have very complex social interactions. And, like only humans and chimpanzees, they recognize themselves in mirrors. In the estuary, you may see them hunting mullet—listen underwater for the clicks. You may also see them playing, leaping from the water or surfing on waves (figure 6.6). These magnificent animals are guaranteed to bring a smile.

Figure 6.6. Leaping bottlenose dolphins (*Tursiops truncatus*). (Photo by Arden Arrington.)

Figure 6.7. Leaping dolphin carved on a wooden tablet, from the Key Marco site. (Watercolor by Wells Sawyer, 1896; photo courtesy of Smithsonian Institution, National Anthropological Archives.)

Judging from an almost complete lack of dolphin remains in Calusa middens, it does not appear that the Calusa ate them or used their bones for tools. We do know that the Calusa enjoyed watching dolphins, however, and perhaps even venerated them, because they depicted dolphins in art. A leaping dolphin carved on a wooden tablet (figure 6.7) and two carved on a piece of bone reflect the beauty of both dolphins and Calusa artwork.

ಚಚಚಚಚಚ

Endangered, Threatened, or Special Concern?

We commonly hear the terms "endangered" and "threatened," but what do they really mean?

An *Endangered Species* faces immediate extinction in the near future and receives the highest level of protection and conservation action by both Florida and U.S. law. (For example, the Florida yew tree, which occurs only in unique ravines in the Florida panhandle, is endangered.)

A *Threatened Species* has a high risk of extinction in the near or short-term future and also receives strong protection from state and federal law to prevent it from becoming endangered. (For example, the bald eagle was once Endangered, but is recovering in numbers and is listed as a Threatened species.)

A *Species of Special Concern* is not in immediate danger of extinction but is protected by Florida law to ensure that it remains secure and does not become at risk for extinction. (For example, the gopher tortoise is listed in Florida as a Species of Special Concern.)

ಚಚಚಚಚಚ

7

𝕆𝕆𝕆𝕆𝕆𝕆

Mangrove Forests

The first-time visitor to a south Florida estuary notices at once the red mangrove trees at the water's edge and their curious arching proproots (figure 7.1). This is a landscape that defined the Calusa domain. They used mangrove wood for firewood, carved it into gauges that helped net-weavers keep the mesh of a fishing net uniform, and may have eaten the young sprouts as emergency foods. Early twentieth century fisherfolk also used mangrove wood for net mesh gauges and net weaving shuttles.

Today Florida mangroves are protected by law, because coastal development once threatened their demise. Mangroves are beautiful to look at but also provide vital services for estuarine residents and for us. Why are mangroves important?

- Mangroves stabilize shorelines and protect the coast from storm surges by breaking the force of high winds and waves.
- Mangrove roots offer shelter to numerous animals, especially when they are young, including many that we like to eat (plate 25). About 75 percent of game fish and 90 percent of commercially harvested sea life depend upon mangroves for food and shelter. Where mangroves have been removed, fish and shellfish populations have seriously declined.
- Mangrove roots are great places for other plants and animals to attach and grow. This includes a whole host of invertebrates that filter the water and keep it clean, such as sponges, oysters, barnacles, and tunicates. As mangrove leaves fall into the water and decay, they provide food for bacteria, fungi, and other organisms, which in turn become food for others.
- Mangroves trap sediments, organic materials, and chemicals and absorb excess nutrients, helping to clarify the water and keep pollutants out of the estuary.
- Mangrove branches serve as nesting sites for coastal birds such as pelicans, roseate spoonbills, herons, white ibis, cormorants, and frigate birds.

Few plants are as well adapted as mangroves to survival amid the tides. These trees tolerate remarkable changes in salinity and water level as the tides go in and out, all the while rooted in essentially anaerobic (lacking oxygen)

Figure 7.1. The proproots of a large red mangrove tree (*Rhizophora mangle*). (Photo by Robert Repenning, courtesy of Florida Department of Environmental Protection.)

mud. Aerial and salt-filtering roots, along with salt-excreting leaves, allow them to occupy saltwater wetlands where other plants cannot survive.

Over four dozen kinds of mangroves occur throughout the world in tropical and subtropical coastal regions. Some grow only in Old World tropics, but others grow worldwide. Florida has three mangrove species, and only south Florida has all three (figure 7.2).

Red mangroves (*Rhizophora mangle*) (figure 7.3) live closest to the water's edge and bear the brunt of storm surges and tidal change. Their unique arched proproots bend but rarely break, easily surviving in high-energy surf. The roots also help the tree survive in oxygen-starved soil by absorbing oxygen through tiny pores. And they combat salt—a huge menace to any plant—by filtering it out right at the root's surface. In the tree canopy, numerous seedlings or propagules hang waiting to fall. When they drop, they may take root in the soft sediments below; or if they hit water, they can float up to 100 days before running aground to take root.

Black mangroves (*Avicennia germinans*) grow on slightly higher ground than do reds. They are easy to recognize by the surrounding mat of finger-like pneumatophores sticking out of the mud (figure 7.4). Like the red mangrove's proproots, pneumatophores enable the black mangrove to take in the oxygen it needs but can't get from the oxygen-poor soil. To combat excess salt, black mangrove leaves have glands that excrete salt onto the leaf where

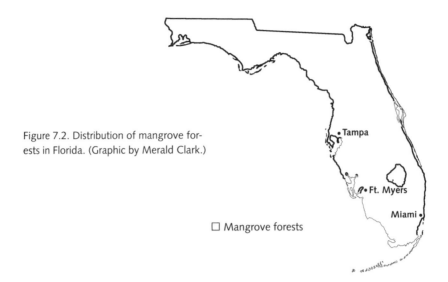

Figure 7.2. Distribution of mangrove forests in Florida. (Graphic by Merald Clark.)

□ Mangrove forests

Figure 7.3. A small red mangrove tree (*Rhizophora mangle*), showing arching proproots and hanging propagules. (Photo by Robert Leavy.)

Figure 7.4. A black mangrove (*Avicennia germinans*) forest with its carpet of pneumato-phores. (Photo by Darcie MacMahon.)

rain can wash it away. In Florida, black mangroves can survive as far north as Cedar Key and sometimes into the Panhandle, but they barely survive the cooler temperatures and often die back in the winter.

White mangroves (*Laguncularia racemosa*) live on the highest ground of all and typically have no visible aerial roots. Like the black mangrove, the white mangrove has special leaf glands to excrete excess salt. Though not much to look at, the flowers of both white and black mangroves attract bees, and mangrove honey is highly prized. White mangroves are easy to identify by their deeply ridged bark, the dimple at the tip of the leaf (figure 7.5), and two salt-excreting glands at the leaf base.

The protection of mangroves is not worldwide. Throughout much of the tropics, mangroves are endangered. Development, forestry, and industry all have big impacts, but the largest threat seems surprising—shrimp farming. Short-lived shrimp ponds have replaced thousands of acres of lush mangrove forests, reducing global mangrove cover by enormous percentages. Shrimp farming not only wipes out mangroves but also devastates the health of estuaries by eliminating habitat for fish and other animals as well as adding huge amounts of excess nutrients and pollution to the water. Reduced biodiversity and a loss of seafood resources are clear results.

Figure 7.5. The leaves of the white mangrove (*Laguncularia racemosa*) have a dimple on the end. (Photo by Darcie MacMahon.)

The south Florida mangrove community hosts a wide variety of vertebrate and invertebrate animals. Some live only in the water, some above the water, and others can survive both in and out of water. Mangrove roots provide anchorage for a huge range of algae and animals and also offer excellent cover for young fish trying to avoid predators. Mangrove treetops host myriad birds and numerous insects. We'll introduce just a few.

Among the Roots

Tunicates: Strange Blobs or Highly Evolved Invertebrates?

If you've never seen a tunicate, they're hard to describe. Depending on the species, tunicates can look like fleshy potatoes, sponges, or odd jellyfish. Contrary to their lumpy appearance, they are in reality one of the most highly evolved of any marine invertebrates, members of the phylum Chordata that contains all animals with spinal chords, including us. Unlike other chordates, the tunicates have a notochord (rudiments of a backbone) and nerve cord only as larvae when they drift about in the sea. As they mature they undergo a drastic metamorphosis, absorbing the notochord and secreting a tough "tunic" or cellulose coat. Tunicates attach to mangrove roots, sea grasses, and other surfaces. All are impressive filter feeders and can clear the water of diatoms, plankton, and suspended particles. You can recognize tunicates by their double siphons—openings that they use to pump water, nutrients, and wastes into and out of their body. Tunicates can also absorb heavy metals and may be useful in handling excess nutrients and pollutants. Other creatures like to live on the tunicates' tough surface, including worms, crabs, amphipods, isopods, and sometimes sea anemones—a veritable grazing ground for fish. Tunicates may also have pharmaceutical uses. Experiments suggest that they have antitumor and antibiotic abilities and may help inhibit certain strains of leukemia.

On south Florida mangrove roots, you will probably find the (lumpy brown) pleated or rough sea squirt (*Styela plicata*), which squirts out a stream of water when threatened. Slightly deeper on the roots or on sea grass leaves are colonies of glass tunicates (*Ecteinascidia turbinata*)—small, delicate, transparent beauties that sometimes have orange rings marking their siphons (plate 26).

Knock, Knock, Anybody Home?

Many insects and some tiny crustaceans cope with the mangrove forest's strong sun and lack of fresh water by living inside mangrove wood. Take, for example, the wood-boring isopod *Sphaeroma terebrans*, a crustacean that burrows into the red mangrove proproots, where it reproduces and matures. At one time scientists believed that the isopods weakened and even killed mangroves; but upon closer inspection others argued that the burrows helped the tree to speed up root production and branching. Another borer, *Coccotrypes rhizophorae*, is a tiny beetle that prefers unhealthy mangroves. It carries into the tree its favorite food—a fungus that prospers on decaying wood and then amply feeds the beetle.

Insects account for about 95 percent of all known animal species on earth and play a vital role in the health of ecosystems. You and I may not enjoy a meal of insects or isopods, but fish and other animals among the mangroves relish these tasty morsels. Even the larva of the dreaded mosquito is a delightful find.

Barnacles: Check Out Those Legs!

Barnacles may look like some sort of mollusk, but they are actually crustaceans related to shrimp and crabs. All of these animals have segmented legs. Barnacles stick theirs in and out of their hard shell casing, frantically beating the water to grab plankton and other passing foods. When the tide goes out, barnacles retreat inside, close a trap-door, and wait for the water to return. Some can remain protected inside for up to a week without drying out. Barnacles are tough stuff. They attach steadfastly to mangrove roots (figure 7.6), pilings, and just about any other available surface, including sea turtles, sea grasses, oysters, and crabs. Look for the different species. On south Florida mangrove roots you may spy the purple stripes of the striped barnacle

Figure 7.6. Striped barnacles (*Balanus amphitrate*) on red mangrove proproots, some with feeding legs extended. (Photo by Robert Repenning, courtesy of Florida Department of Environmental Protection.)

(*Balanus amphitrate*) or the small but tough fragile barnacle (*Chthamalus fragilis*). The Calusa do not appear to have eaten barnacles in their soup. But they make a great snack for hungry black drum fish that nibble with powerful teeth on the barnacles' plated shells.

Anemones: Gardens on the Move

Anemones could be mistaken for strange plants, with their flowery tentacles and bodies attached to other surfaces. But they are actually animals related to corals, and most species can get up and walk around until they find the right spot. Look closely at mangrove roots and you are likely to see the pale or brown anemone (*Aiptasia pallida*). This small animal often lives in groups that resemble exquisite gardens (plate 27). Each anemone has nearly 100 long graceful tentacles that wave about in the water and use stinging cells to stun prey. The pale anemone's brownish color comes from algae that live inside the anemone's body. Through photosynthesis, the algae convert carbon dioxide and water into sugar and oxygen. Both organisms benefit—the algae have a safe home and the anemone extracts nutrients. Anemones may also be nibbled upon and are a favorite food of several sea slugs.

A Shy Crocodile

The words "shy" and "crocodile" don't seem to fit together, but the American crocodile (*Crocodylus acutus*) is indeed a shy reptile. This crocodile lives in coastal areas from Florida to Venezuela and Peru, but populations are now quite small and fragmented. Although they were once common along south Florida's mangrove-fringed estuaries, only about 500 of these endangered animals remain in Florida, at its southernmost tip and the upper Florida Keys (figure 7.7). A long tapering snout and protruding teeth help distinguish the crocodile from its relative the alligator. Did you know that crocodilians are the most vocal of all reptiles and that some can communicate over twenty kinds of messages? Had you heard that crocodiles have glands on their tongue that secrete excess salt and allow them to tolerate saltier water than alligators? They will also drink during a rainstorm by setting their jaws on red mangrove proproots and letting the fresh water run into their mouths. Have you thought of crocs as great mothers? The mom guards her nest of eggs until she hears the babies call. She gently digs them out, carries them in her mouth to the water, and stays nearby to protect them in their first weeks of life.

Figure 7.7. An American crocodile (*Crocodylus acutus*) in a south Florida estuary. (Photo by M. Giannichini, courtesy of Everglades National Park.)

It is not clear from the evidence whether the Calusa hunted crocodiles. They definitely hunted and ate alligators and carved their bones into useful tools and ornaments. The people who lived on Marco Island even carved and painted a beautiful alligator figurehead and painted an alligator-like reptile on a special wooden box. But crocodiles remain elusive in what we know of the Calusa.

Today the endangered American crocodiles need friends. Enjoy learning about them and working to protect them and their mangrove habitats, but please be careful—although generally retiring, the American crocodile is dangerous if surprised or approached and will staunchly protect its nest.

In the Tree Tops

Aerial Acrobat: The Mangrove Crab

Look closely at a mangrove tree and you will surely see the small, well-camouflaged mangrove crab (*Aratus pisonii*) scurrying to hide on the opposite side of the tree (plate 28). Mangrove crabs have legs with needle-like tips and spend much of the day hanging upside-down while clasping roots or branches. When startled, the crab can quickly and securely climb into the treetops, or it may release its grip and plunge into the water below. This escape tactic has flaws. The crab may avoid capture by birds or raccoons but may instead become a snack for passing blue crabs or fish. Mangrove crabs eat fresh red mangrove leaves, but you may also see them scavenging the mud at low tide for algae, small crustaceans, insects, and dead fish. This agile little crab is one of the most abundant residents of the mangrove forest.

The Mangrove Water Snake

The mangrove water snake (*Nerodia fasciata compressicauda*) hunts for food in water but spends much of its time above water wrapped around mangrove roots and branches. If you spot a snake in the mangroves, chances are good that this is your find; but don't count on recognizing its color—this snake can be bright orange, gray, brown, dull yellow, or greenish, and banding marks vary. It hunts at night and often feeds on fish trapped in tidal pools at low tide. The mangrove water snake is not poisonous, but watch out for the teeth. Like all water snakes, its teeth are long and sharp to grasp slippery prey such as fish, shrimp, crabs, tadpoles, and frogs. Worried that poisonous cottonmouth moccasins also like to swim? Unless you know your snakes, it is always a good idea to keep your distance. But you can easily tell the difference between them: water snake eyes can be seen from the top of the head, but a cottonmouth's cannot. Did the Calusa eat this snake? We're not sure. But plenty of other water snakes show up in south Florida middens, so chances are they did (plate 29).

The Mangrove Skipper: Iridescent Blue in a Sea of Green

Skippers are butterflies with robust hairy bodies and triangular wings. The mangrove skipper (*Phocides pigmalion okeechobee*) is one of the largest and most beautiful in Florida (plate 30). When seen among the dark green mangrove leaves, the male's iridescent blue wings are downright spectacular. The less colorful female lays her eggs on red mangrove leaves, and the young caterpillars dine on the leafy greens. Adult mangrove skippers prefer a meal of flower nectar or organic nutrients found in the mud. You may notice male skippers and other male butterflies "puddling" on the sand, drinking up minerals that they pass on to females during mating.

Birds Galore: Mangrove Rookeries

Isolated mangrove islands are well used by nesting birds (figure 7.8). Herons, egrets, spoonbills, wood storks, pelicans, ibis, cormorants, and frigatebirds—all these birds (and more) nest in mangrove trees. What makes mangroves so desirable? Their waterfront location allows birds to hunt nearby; and the broad, sturdy tree canopies easily support many nests. They also provide protection—small mangrove islands support few predators, and their isolated location means few disturbances. Mangrove breeding colonies may host several thousand pairs of various bird species. Most thrive on abundant estuarine foods such as fish, shellfish, and crustaceans. The health of these bird populations is clearly linked to the presence of mangrove forests and a healthy estuarine environment. Enjoy watching rookeries with binoculars, but please don't drive your boat too close. A spooked bird finds it impossible to nest.

Artwork of early south Florida Indian people, much of it quite realistic, features various coastal birds. One look at the Key Marco carved and painted pelican figurehead or the beautifully engraved duck head on a bone pin from the Pineland site makes it clear that the artists were very familiar with birds. Many coastal birds also ended up on Calusa menus, including cormorants, ibis, egrets, and herons. And Calusa people enjoyed adornments of lovely feathers, as have most people worldwide.

a

Figure 7.8. (a) Baby herons on nest. (Photo by Gary Lytton, courtesy of Rookery Bay National Estuarine Research Reserve.) (b) An active bird rookery in southwest Florida and colonial nesters. (Photo by Darcie MacMahon.)

b

Who Needs Glamour to Be Successful?

The mangrove periwinkle (*Littoraria angulifera*), in spite of its sprightly name, is a drab-looking snail (plate 31). Though not much to look at, this small brown snail is highly successful and is one of the most abundant animals in the mangrove forest. Periwinkles live above the high-tide line on red mangrove trees and glide along the tree, scraping off diatoms and microscopic algae with their sharp radula "tongues." Some scientists believe that periwinkles may be evolving from marine to terrestrial snails. While they prefer to be dry, they hang out close to water and can survive being submerged for weeks at a time. Regardless of looks, they are a favorite food for thousands of birds and other wildlife, although the Calusa did not target them for meals.

ⓖⓖⓖⓖⓖⓖ

8

The Bottom Line

When one tugs at a single thing in nature, he finds it attached to the rest of the world.
—John Muir

We have looked at some of the riches of the estuary and explored some of the amazing relationships found there. These relationships are key. No one part of the estuary or any ecosystem exists in a vacuum—all pieces are interrelated in a complex constellation that delights the imagination and enhances the quality of our lives. Indeed, it makes our lives possible as well as pleasurable, from the air we breathe and the water we drink to the food we eat. We are an integral part of our environment, as were the Calusa and their neighbors.

Today some people believe that the world's environmental problems are too complex to understand or too big to do anything about. But this is not really true, for we can all make a difference in spite of the inevitable complexities. The first and most important step is to develop an environmental ethic—an interest in and respect for the natural world, the way it works, and our place in it as well as an interest in living on a healthy planet.

Just as we are all citizens of communities, states, and countries, we are also citizens of the biosphere—the earth's land, water, air, and all living things. The quality of our environment depends on the living ecosystems of the world. If we acknowledge our place in the world, we can begin to make better decisions. The future of Florida's environments is up to us.

Protecting Florida's Estuaries

Modern estuaries face many challenges. Mangroves and sea grasses can recover from natural threats such as hurricanes and can even withstand a fair amount of human abuse. Although estuaries are resilient, they can only stretch so far and may indeed reach the point where recovery from increasing

human threats is difficult if not unlikely unless we reduce the threats. Solutions to many of the problems are far from simple; but the more we understand how things work, the better equipped we are to make decisions.

What are some of the challenges to the estuary? Sometimes dredging and filling in coastal estuaries and bays can directly harm both mangroves and sea grasses. This may leave our coasts vulnerable to damage by storms and our seafood without a diet. The solution is not easy, because dredging also keeps critical waterways open, and filling helps to protect coastal properties. We must support careful analysis of these complex problems and aim to minimize impact on estuaries. We should also support the public purchase of lands to protect these habitats for the future.

Altering rivers and streams can add or subtract fresh water from marine environments. When salt concentrations change too much, animals and plants die, and the ecosystem suffers. Add to this the problem of Florida's shrinking supply of fresh water. Predictions are that Florida will increasingly need to desalinate salt water to make fresh water. What will be the effect on our estuaries? Will the excess salt be dumped in coastal waters—and what will this do? What can we do to conserve fresh water and to reduce fresh water use in agriculture and industry? We must consider the end results of our actions and support sensible regulations.

Figure 8.1. Boat propeller scars through sea grass beds in southwest Florida. (Photo by Corbett Torrence.)

Fertilizers and pesticides from lawns and farms bring a dangerous mix of chemicals into coastal areas. Some are nutrients that drastically alter the habitat, and others are toxins that poison the system. These potent chemicals continue to affect the environment even when they wash into coastal habitats many miles away from their origin. Practices such as integrated pest management and regulation of pollutants may be part of the solution.

Boating, a popular activity nationwide, has skyrocketed in Florida. The number of boat licenses issued in Florida has risen dramatically in recent history. With the increased boating has come more harm to manatees, sea turtles, and other marine life. Boat propellers take their toll on both animals and sea grasses, and carelessly dropped anchors damage sea grasses too (figure 8.1). In addition, some scientists believe that the increase in activity and the noise from boats prevent some fish from reproducing. While regulating the number of boats on the water is difficult, we can all work to minimize the impact of our own boating habits and encourage others to do the same. For something different, try kayaks or canoes. Support the replanting of sea grasses and help protect sea-grass beds from further destruction.

The number of people fishing is greater than ever, as is the efficiency with which they can locate and capture their quarry. Fish and shellfish are now under a double threat—habitat destruction and over-fishing. The long-term health of Florida's marine resources depends on protection of the physical environment and controls on the removal of fish and shellfish from the sea.

ⓖⓖⓖⓖⓖⓖ

9

The Fishing Heritage
of Gulf Coastal Florida

The Calusa prospered from the amazing bounty of the estuary. Their food, their art, and probably their religion and politics were woven into the fabric of life on the estuary (figure 9.1). Their staple diet of fish and shellfish was directly dependent on the health of the estuarine system, and their population was small enough that these resources were never seriously affected. Many of their fishing traditions survive today. Let's look at what we know about early fishing in Florida.

The First Coastal Dwellers

We can only speculate about the first people who lived on Florida's coastal estuaries, because the places where they would have lived are now under many feet of water. Indian people lived in interior Florida by 12,000 years ago. Even though Florida was cooler and drier then, it stands to reason that some of these early Floridians also lived on or near the coast, where creeks and streams reached the sea. But Florida's coastline was much farther out at that time because sea level was lower. Therefore, any evidence of coastal peoples before about 6,000–4,000 years ago, when sea level reached its current height, is now deep under the sea (figure 9.2). The only exceptions are settlements built high atop ancient dune ridges that accumulated during the Pleistocene, such as Horr's Island in Collier County and Useppa Island in Lee County. These sites preserve evidence that people prospered from a fishing economy as early as 6,000 years ago.

If people fished along Florida's Gulf coast 6,000 years ago, were they Calusa? The Calusa were the most powerful of all known native peoples along the Gulf coast, but their culture can be traced with confidence only to about A.D. 500—about 1,500 years ago—on the southwest Florida coast. Perhaps the earlier coastal people were direct ancestors of the Calusa, but maybe not. We do know that by the sixteenth century A.D. the Calusa controlled the

Figure 9.1. Artist's conception of a Calusa fishing village. (Drawing by Merald Clark.)

ⓑⓑⓑⓑⓑⓑ

Sea Level Fluctuations

Why was the ocean so much lower 12,000 years ago than it is today? The answer has to do with the earth's fluctuating climate. As global climate changes, sea level responds. In colder times seawater freezes at the north and south poles, so sea level falls. As the earth warms up again, the polar ice melts and sea level rises. When the most recent Ice Age ended about 12,000 years ago, the oceans rose accordingly. By 6,000 to 4,000 years ago the rising sea had defined Florida's modern coastline.

There have been short-term variations in sea level, too. For example, about 1,600 years ago a warm period may have caused waters to rise to four feet above today's level in southwest Florida. Indian people moved inland in response. Today scientists believe that the sea is rising by 0.06 to 0.12 inches per year. At that rate, the Gulf of Mexico will be five to ten feet higher by the year 3000 than it is today.

Scientists agree that today's sea level is higher than it was 12,000 years ago, but they disagree about the way it has risen. Some feel that sea level slowly but steadily rose to its present position with only a few interruptions but was never higher than today's level. Others think that there have been many fluctuations within the overall trend toward a higher level, a few of which attained a height above today's level.

ⓑⓑⓑⓑⓑⓑ

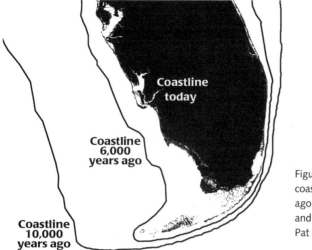

Figure 9.2. South Florida coastline at 10,000 years ago, 6,000 years ago, and today. (Graphic by Pat Payne.)

entire southern half of Florida. They traveled far by canoe, engineering canals to connect coastal towns to inland waterways and communities. They were fishing people who prospered from the immense bounty of their coastal world. Although the Calusa are gone, many of their ancient fishing traditions continue to the present day along the Florida Gulf coast.

Fishing on the Gulf Coast of Florida

Foods from the Estuary

The contents of old garbage dumps called middens tell us what the Calusa ate. The bones and shells are identified by zooarchaeologists, the seed and wood remains by archaeobotanists. The Calusa depended on the estuary for most of their food (figure 9.3). They ate pinfish, grunt, mullet, sheepshead, and catfish as well as oysters, clams, whelks, and conchs. Less common but perhaps more valued were seatrout, redfish, grouper, snapper, snook, and shark. The Calusa did not farm staple crops such as corn, although they did keep small household gardens. They also hunted animals and gathered dozens of different wild plants for food and medicine.

More Than Just Food

The Calusa found many ways to use the bones, teeth, and shells of sea creatures. Take sharks, for example. They used shark teeth to make precision cutting and drilling tools and deadly weapons (plate 32, figure 9.4). The oil from

Dependable Fish

What sizes of fish make the most reliable catch for everyday meals?

- Big fish? Great to eat! But depending on big fish is risky. They can be hard to catch and can break nets and fishing lines.
- Medium fish? Some are a good bet. Sea catfish are plentiful and easy to catch on a hook or in nets. Mullet are easy to net in winter when they gather to spawn.
- Small fish? Best all-around daily food. Small fish are almost always available and can be caught in large numbers with nets or traps. These were a staple food of the Calusa.

ⓑⓑⓑⓑⓑⓑ

shark livers could be mixed with pigments to make a body paint that also repelled mosquitoes. Rough shark skin created a perfect sandpaper, because tiny tooth-like scales, called *denticles*, make the skin rough. The tips of shark teeth, removed from the whole teeth and trimmed, could be inserted into boards and used to grate roots (figure 9.5).

Shellfish are another good example. The Calusa enjoyed eating oysters, clams, and conchs, as many people do today. But the Calusa were also experts

Figure 9.3. Artist's conception of a Calusa meal. (Drawing by Merald Clark.)

Figure 9.4. A Calusa man carves a wooden mask with shark-tooth tools. (Drawing by Merald Clark.)

Figure 9.5. A Calusa woman grates roots on a shark-tooth grater board. (Drawing by Merald Clark.)

ᭊᭊᭊᭊᭊᭊ

The Calusa Rewrite History

Scholars long believed that all politically and socially complex societies raised some staple crop, such as corn or manioc. But the Calusa and people like them demonstrate that societies can be highly complex, powerful, and artistic without depending on farming for their main food supply. The Calusa had small gardens, but their main staple food was fish (figure 9.6).

ᭊᭊᭊᭊᭊᭊ

Figure 9.6. A Calusa man returns from a day's fishing. (Drawing by Merald Clark.)

at making tools from their shells. They chose the right shells for the right jobs, such as horse-conch sinkers, lightning-whelk hammers, and clam-shell knives (plate 33).

Figure 9.7. Calusa women pull a seine net. (Drawing by Merald Clark.)

Nets of Plenty

Nets were the foundation of Calusa success. For a society built on fishing, nets provided daily sustenance. The Calusa made cord nets with different-sized openings (meshes) to catch fish of different sizes and changed nets by season as fish grew larger. They probably used dip nets near shore and from boats, seine and gill nets in shallow waters (figure 9.7) and stop nets to trap fish as the tide went out.

The Calusa constructed nets of palm-fiber cord (figure 9.8). They made standard-sized meshes by knotting the cord around rectangular gauges (figure 9.9). The knot they used, a sheet bend, is still used today for making nets. Cypress-wood pegs and hollow gourds kept the top of the net afloat. Shells and stones weighed down the bottom (plate 34). Netting technology changed very little until the mid twentieth century.

Cord for fishing nets and line could be made from many different plants (figure 9.10). The fiber from cabbage-palm leaves and saw-palmetto trunks can be spun into yarn and twisted into cord. Century plants yield long fibers

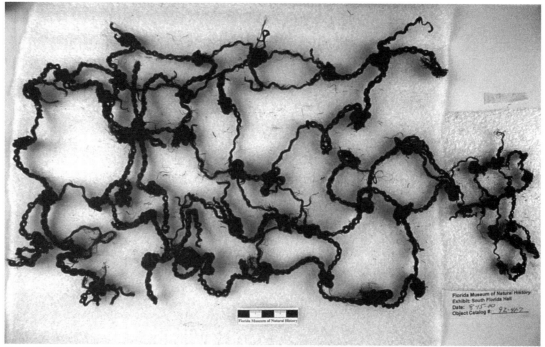

Figure 9.8. Palm-fiber fish net fragment from the Key Marco site. (Photo by Jeff Gage.)

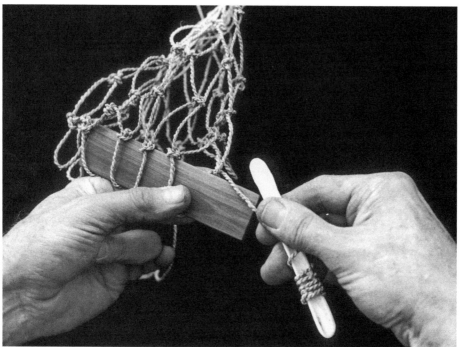

Figure 9.9. Close-up photo showing weaving of a palm-fiber net. (Photo by Robin Brown.)

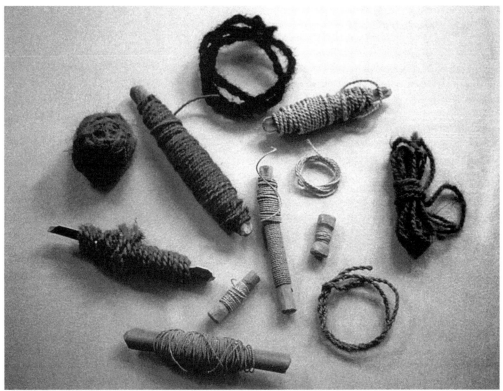

Figure 9.10. Fibers used for cordage. Outer group, clockwise from top: Spanish moss, four-ply rope (*Tillandsia usneoides*); mulberry bark, two-ply rope (*Morus rubra*); cabbage palm (*Sabal palmetto*), trunk fiber, two-ply rope; cypress bark, two-ply rope (*Taxodium ascendens*, pond, or *distichum*, bald); cabbage palm leaf, split fiber, two-ply cord; saw palmetto, trunk fiber, two-ply rope (*Serenoa repens*); cabbage palm, trunk fiber, spun yarn; cabbage palm, trunk fiber, two-ply cord (*Sabal palmetto*). Inner group: upper right coil is willow bark, two-ply cord (*Salix caroliniana*); long spool is cabbage palm leaf, split fiber, two-ply cord (*Sabal palmetto*); two short spools are century plant fiber, two-ply cord and thread (*Agave decipiens*). (Photo and cordage reproductions by Robin Brown.)

that can be twisted into strong twine. The inner bark of some trees can be peeled into small strips to make cord. Even dried Spanish moss yields a curly black fiber that can be made into rope.

Other Ways to Catch a Fish

There are many ways to catch a fish. The Calusa used nets most often. But they also fished with spears, hooks, composite hooks, throat gorges, and probably weirs and traps (figures 9.11 and 9.12). On the southeastern Florida coast in 1696, Philadelphian Jonathan Dickinson observed one Indian fishing technique:

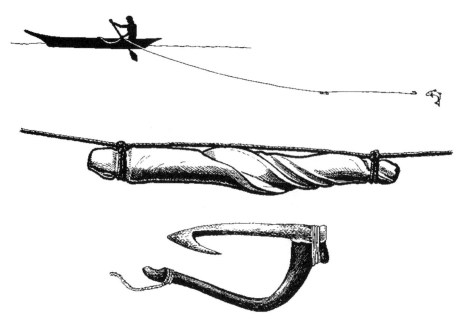

Figure 9.11. Other ways to catch fish: (top) sinker made from shell; (bottom) composite fishhook made of carved bone, wood, and twine. (Drawings by Merald Clark, graphic by Pat Payne.)

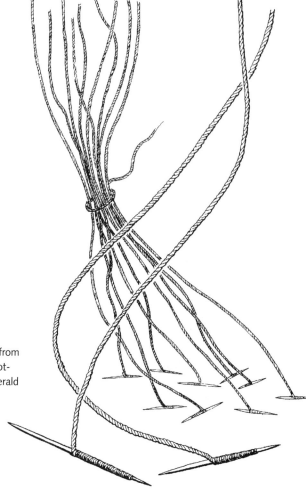

Figure 9.12. Throat gorges made from deer bone were baited to catch bottom-feeding fish. (Drawing by Merald Clark.)

This morning the Caseekey [the principal leader] . . . sent his son with his striking staff to the inlet to strike fish for us; which was performed with great dexterity; . . . though we looked very earnestly when he threw his staff, [we] could not see a fish at which time he saw it, and brought it on shore on the end of his staff. Sometimes he would run swiftly pursuing a fish, and seldom missed when he darted at him. In two hours time he got as many fish as would serve twenty men. (Dickinson 1985)

The Mighty Canoe

Canoes were vital to Calusa life. They were used for everyday travel, trade, fishing, and warfare. To date, no one has found an actual Calusa canoe, but they probably made dugout canoes from the same trees used by other Florida Indian peoples—pine and cypress. To shape the boat, they burned the middle and chopped out the charred wood with robust shell tools. They used other shell tools to finish the surfaces.

Canoes for calm water had simple prows, and those for rougher seas had projecting prows (figure 9.13). To carry big loads, they made barges by lashing a platform between two canoes. Smaller canoes could be pulled as dinghies. And the Calusa even made canoe-shaped bowls and toys.

Figure 9.13. A Calusa boy watches a canoe pass in a village canal (note projecting prow and stern). (Drawing by Merald Clark.)

Figure 9.14. Artist's conception of the Calusa leader's canoe, based on descriptions in Spanish documents. In the foreground, commoners unload daily catch from a canoe barge as children play with toy canoes. (Drawing by Merald Clark.)

When the Calusa leader traveled, he had his own special double canoe, with a sheltered platform on which he sat (figure 9.14). Gonzalo Solís de Merás, nephew and secretary of Spanish Florida's governor Pedro Menéndez, observed this impressive scene in 1566: "Within two hours [came the leader], with as many as twelve canoes, and two of them fastened one to the other, with decks covered with awnings of hoops and matting" (Solís de Merás 1964).

ⓖⓖⓖⓖⓖⓖ

10

The Calusa

Two major sources provide information about the Calusa and their neighbors. First, Spanish and other European documents of the period 1566–1760 record certain details about Calusa towns and the people who lived there, including some of their customs, spiritual beliefs, and political practices. Second, archaeology reveals details about Calusa life—the tools that they made and used, foods they ate, their artistic expression, and much more (figures 10.1, 10.2). In this chapter we describe what is known of Calusa society using both kinds of information.

Calusa Society

Where Did They Come From?

The exact origins of the Calusa people are not precisely known. As we have seen, the fishing tradition of Gulf coastal Florida goes back at least 6,000 years. We don't know whether the Calusa people described by the Spaniards in the 1500s and 1600s were direct descendants of these ancient fisherfolk. We do not believe that the Calusa people came from any great distance away, and we have found no artifacts that would suggest that they migrated into south Florida from, say, Mexico or the Caribbean. But how long were the Calusa in south Florida, and where did their ancestors come from?

To tell whether a distinct group of people has been in a place for a long time, archaeologists study the *material culture* (the pottery, shell, bone, stone, and other artifacts that the people left behind) and look for change through time. If they detect only gradual changes through time, this favors the idea that a single group was in an area for a long period. A sudden change in styles of tools, pottery, art, or weaponry, however, tends to argue for one group of people being replaced by a distinctly different group, perhaps by warfare or in-migration.

In the case of southwest Florida—the Calusa heartland—we can certainly say that fishing was an established way of life early on and that it continued

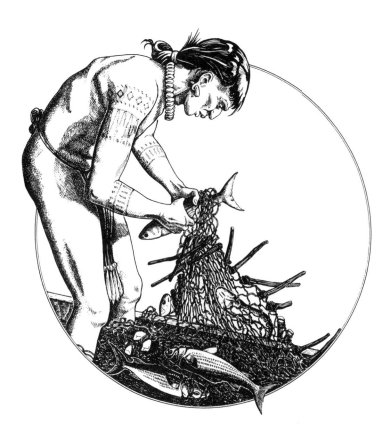

Figure 10.1. A Calusa man pulls mullet from a net. We know about Calusa fishing traditions from both archaeology and historical documents. (Drawing by Merald Clark.)

y no dire mas por que si fuera pretender la conquista de esta tierra
no diera mas relazion que tengo dado aunque a su mag.d
le conbiene para la seguridad de sus armadas que ban al peru
y a la nueba españa y otras partes de yndias que pasan
por fuerza por aquella costa y canal de bahama y se pierden
muchos nabios y pere se mucha gente porque los yndios son
contrarios y muy flecheros y ansi como digo conbiene a bez
alguna fuerza se hubiera por do pudiesen segurar aquella canal
con alguna renta que se pudiese sacar de mexico y del peru
y de las yslas de cuba y de todas partes de yndias para
el remedio y mantenim.to de los soldados de guarda
fuerza ... es lo que conbenia y otra cosa mas
de ir a buscar las perlas pues esta riquesa no ai en a
quella tierra y para ello conduxo y si fuere nesesario

lo firmo do de escalante fontaneda

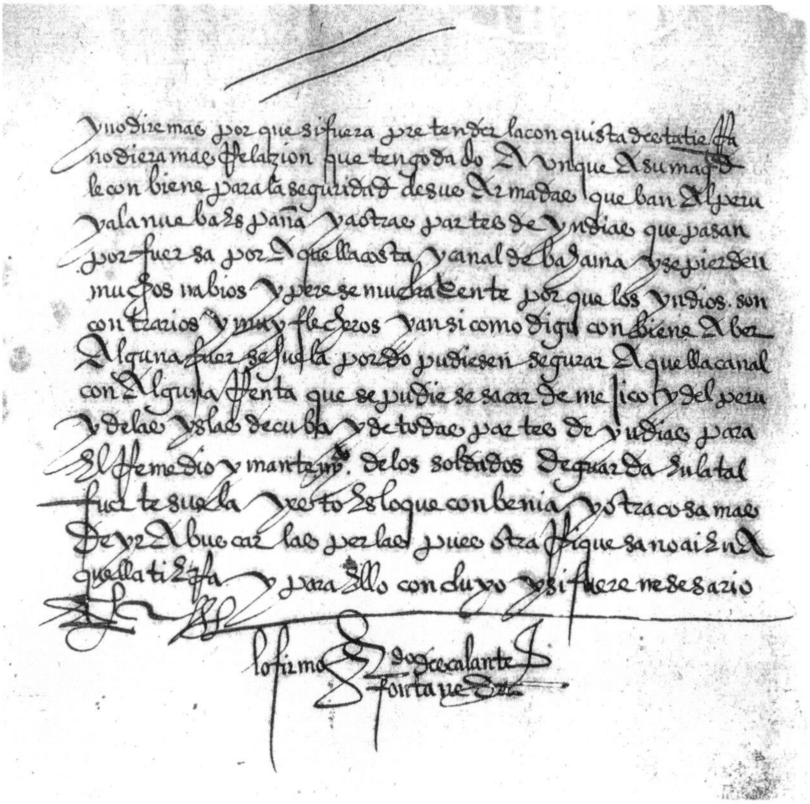

Figure 10.2. Spanish documents such as this page from Hernando de Escalante Fontaneda's manuscript about his captivity in Florida help shed light on Calusa life. (Courtesy of Special Collections, University of Florida Libraries.)

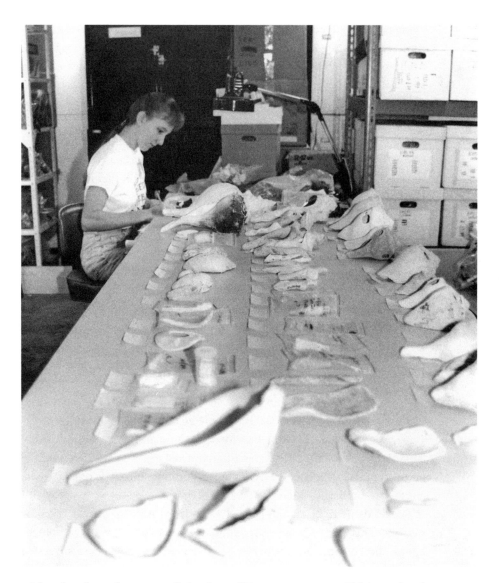

with only minor changes until the time of European contact. Fishing-related artifacts such as nets, traps, and spears changed slowly. There is great similarity in the basic enterprise: net-fishing and shellfish gathering, supplemented by the use and limited cultivation of plants (the latter by at least 2,000 years ago). Stone and shell tool styles also reflect trends across a wide area of Florida (figure 10.3).

In the everyday pottery of southwest Florida we can detect a noticeable change between A.D. 200 and 500. Prior to about A.D. 500, people of the southwest coast made plain (that is, undecorated) pottery using clay tempered with sand. Archaeologists call this pottery "Sand-tempered Plain." (Temper is material added to the clay to make it more easily shaped by human hands and less likely to crack when fired.) About A.D. 200 to 300, people

Figure 10.3. Carol Godwin catalogues shell artifacts from southwest Florida. Changes in artifact styles can help archaeologists track movements of people and ideas through time. (Photo by William Marquardt.)

living near Lake Okeechobee began to use a clay high in sponge spicules—tiny, needle-like structures that are found naturally in freshwater sponges. Archaeologists call this kind of pottery "Belle Glade Plain," named after an archaeological site near Lake Okeechobee.

By A.D. 500, the people on the coast had begun to make or use plain pottery very similar to that of the Belle Glade people at Okeechobee; and by A.D. 1000, it was the most common kind of pottery made in both areas. This could mean several things: (1) that people living on the coast began to trade more actively with people around Lake Okeechobee; (2) that the Okeechobee-area people migrated to the southwest Florida coast, conquering or simply amalgamating with the coastal folk; or (3) that the coastal people were so impressed with the Belle Glade pottery that they began to make their pottery the same way, using the same raw materials. In any case, the pottery on the coast—the area that would become the Calusa heartland—did not change radically after about A.D. 500. We feel comfortable in saying that the people encountered by the Spaniards in the 1500s descended from people who had lived on the southwest Florida coast for at least 1,000 years (that is, from at least A.D. 500) but perhaps much longer.

Leadership

Spanish documents say the Calusa people believed that their leader, or cacique, was responsible for the bounty of the land and waters. (*Cacique* is a Taino Indian word that the Spaniards adopted and used for various village and paramount chiefs in the New World.) Calusa leaders were kin to one another and inherited their positions.

Spaniards described Calusa society as divided into "nobles" and "commoners." This surprises some contemporary Indian people, who do not recognize such distinctions in their tribes today. Some people have suggested that because Spanish society was organized into nobles and commoners at the time, the Spaniards may have misinterpreted what they saw. But when all the historical documents are taken together, it seems clear that a small group of powerful leaders made decisions for the Calusa and provided protection and that the majority of the people supplied food for the leaders and labor for public works projects (figure 10.4).

The cacique, a spiritual leader, and a military captain were the three primary leaders. The Calusa leader sat on a special stool and was greeted with ceremony by his subjects. One account mentions processions of masked priests, accompanied by women singing. Masks covered the inner walls of a "temple."

The Spanish documents say that the cacique was expected to marry his sister and that the cacique's son generally succeeded him. It is possible that

Figure 10.4. A large labor force was required to construct and maintain Calusa canals. This is an artist's conception of the Pine Island canal. (Drawing by Merald Clark.)

the Spaniards misunderstood the Calusa, who may have meant that the cacique was expected to marry within his own clan: that is, to marry a cousin or "clan sister." In any case, the Calusa leader had numerous wives. South Florida Indian people formalized alliances by providing a woman to be married to the Calusa paramount leader.

The Calusa Name

Europeans attributed various names to the Calusa, including Carlos, Calos, Caloosa, and Caalus. For example, Hernando de Escalante Fontaneda wrote in 1575 that "Carlos in their language signifies a fierce people. They are so-called for being brave and skillful, as in truth they are" (Fontaneda 1944). The Calusa may have used a different name for themselves. Many Indian groups simply call themselves "The People" in their own language.

Spaniards called the Calusa leader "Carlos" (Spanish for "Charles"), but this was apparently a mispronunciation of a Calusa word. In 1562 Frenchman René de Laudonnière wrote the name as "Calos" (figure 10.5). Spanish Jesuit missionary Juan Rogel reported in 1567 that "Caalus, which the Spaniards mispronouncing the word called him Carlos . . . is the greatest of the caciques that there is in all this coast of Florida" (Hann 1991).

All the accounts agree that at the time of European contact the Calusa were the most powerful people in all of south Florida. Tribes from as far away as present-day Cape Canaveral, Lake Okeechobee, Miami, and the Florida Keys allied themselves with the Calusa cacique.

The Calusa Capital

The Spaniards describe "Calos" as the Calusa capital town, located on an island in the middle of a bay, two day's sail from Havana. In a 1575 account, Hernando de Escalante Fontaneda refers to this bay as "the bay of Carlos," but he notes that it was called Escampaba in the language of the Indians. This is probably the same place noted on the count of Ottomanno Freducci's map of 1514–15 as Stababa, shown at Estero Bay near present-day Fort Myers Beach (figure 10.6). The Freducci map was based on information from the 1513 voyage of Ponce de León, suggesting that his engagement with the Calusa occurred at or near there. Based on Spanish accounts, the main town of the Calusa was probably located on Mound Key in Estero Bay (near Fort Myers Beach). Thus "Escampaba" probably refers to today's Estero Bay.

The Jesuit mission of San Antón de Carlos was established at Calos in 1567 in the "court of the kings," the precinct where the Calusa nobles lived. Apparently the Spanish entourage occupied some three dozen Indian houses. Assuming that the Calusa capital town was the same place over a century later, the 1697 Franciscan mission of San Diego de Compostela may have been in the same area, because the church was built near the house of the Calusa leader. In 1697 the population of the island was about 1,000.

Calusa Connections: Trade, Exchange, and Tribute

The Calusa traded and communicated with other Indian people throughout eastern North America. Ancient networks supplied the Calusa with exotic materials such as stone and minerals in exchange for large seashells and other local goods (figure 10.7). Materials and products from afar came to the Calusa in various ways—through trade, exchange, and tribute.

Trade was commonly carried out through barter, as people met to swap things they had for things they needed. True money, in the form of a currency recognized over vast regions, did not exist.

Like trade, exchange involves the transfer of items between individuals, but it is a transfer with strong social or ritual meanings. The goods themselves may be special or ritual objects that serve to cement political or social

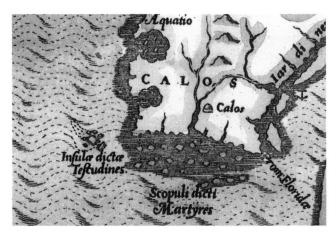

Figure 10.5. This antique French map, though inaccurate in detail, places the province and capital of Calos in south Florida. (Courtesy of Special Collections, University of Florida Libraries.)

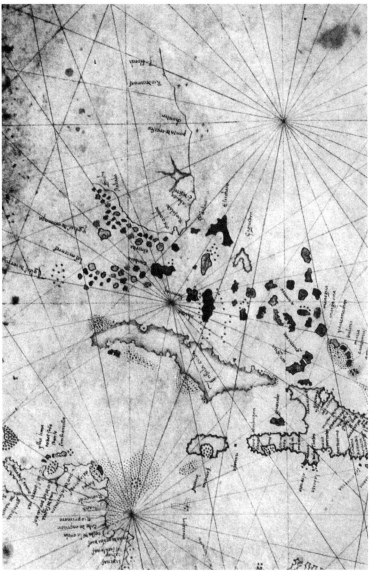

Figure 10.6. The Freducci map, based on Ponce de León's first voyage, is the earliest detailed map of coastal south Florida. (Courtesy of Archivo di Stato, Firenze, Italy.)

relationships. Such exchanges of items may occur at diplomatic occasions, such as conferences between leaders; or the ritualized exchange of items may precede other events, such as a marriage or a ceremony of alliance. Exchange implies reciprocity, but sometimes the giving of a special item cannot be reciprocated. A modern example is the small fragments of moon rocks presented by the United States to foreign governments in the 1970s. When a leader can give a gift that no one else can, it tends to demonstrate his or her power.

Tribute is an obligatory payment of goods or services in order to demonstrate allegiance. In the 1560s Spanish records indicate that the Calusa leader controlled over fifty towns and that many other towns paid tribute to him. Items of tribute brought to the Calusa leader included foods, mats, hides, feathers, plunder from shipwrecks, and sometimes captive people. Although captives were put to work, there is no evidence that the Calusa had large numbers of slaves. Spaniards wrote that the Calusa killed some captives; but we know that not all were killed because in 1566 some captive Spanish women chose to stay with their Spanish-Indian children rather than leave with the Spaniards. One captive Spaniard, Escalante Fontaneda, lived among the Calusa for seventeen years before returning to Spain.

All three processes—trade, exchange, and tribute—can move items from place to place, sometimes surprising distances (plate 35). For example, a lump of galena (lead ore) found at the Pineland Site Complex and dating to about A.D. 1250 can be traced to present-day southeast Missouri, a distance of over 1,000 miles. Galena was traded widely throughout the eastern United States beginning over 2,000 years ago. Indian people in the American Midwest pounded galena into glitter and used it to make face and body paint. Perhaps the Calusa used galena in a similar way. People also traded large lightning whelk shells long distances, from the Gulf coast as far away as present-day Oklahoma, Kentucky, New York, and North Dakota. The Calusa were probably involved in this movement of shells.

Calusa Beliefs

In spite of the abundance the Calusa enjoyed, the Spaniards reported that they were intrigued by European foods, wine, clothing, and metals. But one part of their culture that the Calusa maintained strongly was their belief system. Spaniards tried to convert the Calusa to Catholicism. They preached to them, bribed them, and threatened them; but the Calusa remained faithful to their centuries-old convictions. Juan Rogel, a Spanish missionary who lived among the Calusa, recorded some of their fundamental beliefs in 1567:

They say that each person has three souls. One is the little pupil of the eye; another is the shadow that each one casts; and the last is the image of oneself that each one sees in a mirror or in a calm pool of water. And when a person dies, they say that two of the souls leave the body and that the third one, which is the pupil of the eye, remains in the body always. And thus they go to the burial place to speak with the deceased ones and to ask their advice. . . . From what the deceased say to them there they learn about many things that happen in other regions or that come to pass later on. (Hann 1991) (figure 10.8)

They believe those who govern the world to be three persons. . . . The first one, who is greater than the other two, is the one to whom the universal government of the most universal and common things belongs, such as the heavenly movements and the seasons. . . . The second one is greater than the third, that to him belongs the government of the kingdoms, empires, and republics. The third one, who is the least of all and the one who helps in the wars. And to the side to which he attaches himself, they say that that one gains victory. (Hann 1991)

The Calusa say that when a person dies, the soul enters into some animal or fish. And when they kill such an animal, it enters into another lesser one so that little by little it reaches the point of being reduced into nothing. (Hann 1991)

Figure 10.7. Places of origin for some materials found on Calusa sites. (Map by Merald Clark.)

Figure 10.8. The Calusa believed that each person has three souls. (Painting by Merald Clark.)

The quickly changing political world of Spanish colonial Florida must have been an enormous challenge for the Calusa. Spanish accounts refer to the Calusa as a "fierce people." Certainly they resisted Spanish attempts to control them, and they succeeded for over 200 years in spite of the power of Spanish weapons and the coercion of Spanish priests. This confounded the Spaniards, as missionary Juan Rogel related:

> They said to me that their forbears had lived under this law from the beginning of time and that they also wanted to live under it, that I should let them be, that they did not want to listen to me. (Hann 1991)

The spiritual and the material realms made up one seamless world for south Florida native people. According to documents, common people believed in the absolute power of the Calusa leader. His power was a function of—and proof of—his identification with both the practical and the spiritual features of their everyday world. As their leader prospered, the land and the waters would continue to bring forth their abundance. His struggles, his wars and alliances, and his dealings with the spirits of the dead were in the interests of all; and whatever he required of them had to be given without question. Spiritual authority and political authority, easily discussed separately in our society, were for the Calusa one and the same.

To separate the Calusa leader from the spiritual world was to destroy him as an authority figure and deny him his reason for existence. Political authority and spiritual knowledge went hand in hand, as revealed in this observation by Jesuit missionary Juan Rogel, who here refers to the cacique or paramount leader as "the king":

> It is expedient for him to show to his vassals and to his neighboring kings that he is the legitimate king of this kingdom and because to that end during his childhood they taught and instructed him in all the things that it is expedient for the king to know about the cult and veneration of the idols, if he were suddenly to forsake the idolatry at the beginning of his reign, the aforementioned kings and vassals would say that he was not a legitimate king, as he did not know what kings are obliged to know. (Hann 1991)

Thus, Calusa beliefs, tied closely to political authority, were integral to Calusa society. The Calusa steadfastly refused to accept Spanish beliefs and Spanish authority, successfully resisting European intrusion for nearly 200 years after Ponce de León's first incursion.

Calusa Ceremonies

Calusa people had time for games, song, dance, and public ceremonies. Some of these were apparently serious occasions, such as the procession of masked priests, accompanied by singing women (although it is obvious from the descriptions that the Spaniards had no respect for Calusa beliefs and ceremonies). In 1607 Juan Sánchez commented on the events he witnessed in 1567:

> While the said father [Rogel] was there, a notable thing happened. And it was that [there] was a temple of idols there, [in] which were some very ugly masks, which some Indians donned, delegated by it. And they went out into the village with them. And the wretches performed their worship and adored them, with the women singing certain canticles. (Hann 1991)

In 1567 Juan Rogel wrote:

> . . . they attempted to climb up to our fort to hold a procession with their masks, coming from a little hill, where they had their houses, to the hill on which our fort was located. Between these hills there was a little valley where they were accustomed to promenade in view of the people. . . . And the women adored them and sang their praises. (Hann 1991)

Dramatizing a Chiefly Meeting

The Solís de Merás account inspired our dramatization of a meeting between Caalus and Tequesta in the Florida Museum of Natural History's Hall of South Florida (plate 36). In the dramatized scene, the Calusa leader Caalus and his closest advisors welcome the visiting leader. It is 1564 in the Calusa capital town of Calos, on today's Mound Key near Fort Myers. The visiting leader has traveled from the Tequesta region (today's Miami area) to bring news from a distant realm of the Calusa domain. In the traditional way, Tequesta offers his hands palm up as a sign of respect. Caalus will touch Tequesta's hands to acknowledge the greeting. Also represented in the re-created scene are the spiritual leader, Caalus's father; the military leader, Caalus's cousin, whom the Spaniards called "Felipe"; Caalus's principal wife; and Caalus's sister, whom the Spaniards called "Antonia"; she would later be married to Pedro Menéndez in an unsuccessful attempt to cement an alliance between the Spaniards and the Calusa.

In conceiving this scene, we wanted to provide the opportunity for our visitors to visualize specific Calusa people at a certain historical time and also to display some of the known facts about them. We don't know exactly what the Calusa looked like, but history and archaeology have given us some clues. We know that the Calusa and their neighbors spent time on personal adornment and used it to signify status and mark ceremonies as well as to enjoy beauty. Archaeologists have recovered various adornments and pigments that may have been used for body paint (plates 37 and 38). Documents describe some body paint practices and occasionally mention dress, jewelry, and other ornamentation.

For example, in 1566 a Spaniard described Caalus's principal wife thus:

> His wife . . . was 20 years old, very comely and beautiful, . . . her eyebrows were very well marked, and she wore at her throat a very beautiful collar of pearls and stones and a necklace of gold beads. (Solís de Merás 1964)

Body paint was very important to the Calusa, judging from Spanish descriptions:

> [The leader] stains himself black on his face and on his body. (Hann 1991)

> The men paint themselves variously almost every day, a custom they practice, we have learned, for the honor of the principal idol that they venerate. (Hann 1991)

Archaeologists have recovered other evidence of body ornamentation—a startling variety of ornaments, pigments that could have been used for body paint, and at least one possible tattoo needle made of bone. The Spaniards never mention tattooing, however, so the bone needle may have had other purposes. At the Key Marco site, Cushing found another clue to Calusa appearance—a tiny portrait of a man painted on the inside of a clam shell (figure 10.9).

Modern experiments with minerals and native plant pigments, such as those by Robin Brown, also contribute information about the types and colors of pigments and dyes available to the Calusa. By combining these clues, we can begin to imagine the appearance of the Calusa and to understand their concepts of beauty.

ᘐᘐᘐᘐᘐᘐᘐ

Figure 10.9. A clam shell from the Key Marco site with the image of a man painted inside. Shell is 3½ inches high. (Computer-enhanced image by Merald Clark.)

Another account by Hernando de Escalante Fontaneda suggests that people impersonating spirits spent weeks at a time in Calusa towns:

> After the summer come some sorcerers in the shape of the devil with some horns on their heads, and they come howling like wolves and many other different idols which yell like animals of the woods, and these idols stay four months, in which they never rest night or day, running so much with great fury. (Worth 1995)

One detailed account of a ceremony of allegiance was provided by Gonzalo Solís de Merás, nephew and secretary of Spanish Florida's governor, Pedro Menéndez de Avilés. It concerned a meeting between Governor Menéndez and Calusa paramount leader Caalus in February 1566. The meeting must have been quite a sight to see. The Calusa nobility were painted colorfully and dressed in their finest clothing. Hundreds of people of all ages stood outside the Calusa leader's great house, which Solís de Merás tells us was so large that 2,000 people could gather inside without being crowded.

Menéndez's entrance was also dramatic. He was accompanied by 200 soldiers carrying *arquebuses* (portable matchlock cannons), a flag-bearer, several musicians playing fifes, trumpets, drums, and a psaltery (a stringed instrument), and a dwarf who was a great singer and dancer. Menéndez entered Caalus's house with 20 of his party, and the soldiers waited outside. In a large room he found the Calusa leader sitting on a raised seat, accompanied by his wife, who was sitting slightly lower. Around them were 500 men and 500 women.

Caalus professed his allegiance to Menéndez and offered him his sister as a wife, according to Calusa custom. Then a celebration began. Five hundred teenaged girls sang outside the window, then the people inside the house sang and danced. The Spaniards and Indians exchanged gifts, food was brought out by both, and the Spanish musicians entertained. Neither the marriage of Caalus's sister to the governor nor the political alliance between the Spaniards and the Calusa ultimately lasted, but the description of this ceremony gives us some insight into Calusa political structure and customs.

Calusa Hospitality

At diplomatic occasions, the Calusa served food and drink. They drank teas made from various plants and often dined on wild fruits and roots. Archaeological evidence indicates that although there was no full-scale agriculture, the Calusa grew garden crops such as papayas, chile peppers, and squash. Offerings to spirits of the dead included tobacco, and it may have been used on other occasions.

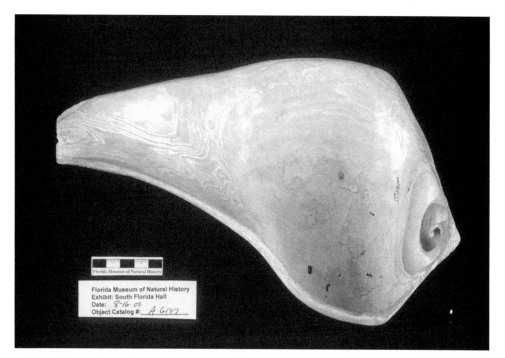

Figure 10.10. A polished lightning-whelk vessel from the Key Marco site. (Photo by Jeff Gage.)

Sometimes the Calusa ate meats of deer, turtle, and duck, but fish and shellfish were their daily staples. In fact, when Menéndez met Caalus in 1566, the Calusa leader "ordered the food to be brought, which consisted of many kinds of very good fish, roasted and boiled; and oysters, raw, boiled and roasted" (Solís de Merás 1964). Additional insight is provided by Fontaneda:

> The common food is fish, turtle, and snails (all of which are alike fish), and tunny [tuna] and whale. . . . Some eat sea-wolves [seals]; not all of them, for there is a distinction between the higher and the lower classes, but the principal persons eat them. (Fontaneda 1944)

One Calusa drink was probably cassina, or yaupon holly tea, which was consumed throughout the southeastern United States to achieve purity and social harmony. High in caffeine, the tea was also valued as a stimulant. It was often served in lightning-whelk drinking vessels (figure 10.10). The plant (*Ilex vomitoria*) grew in coastal settings along the Gulf and Atlantic coasts but was traded inland and used throughout the interior Southeast. Englishman James Adair commented on its widespread use:

> The Yopon [tea], or Cusseena, is very plenty, as far as the salt air reaches over the low lands. It is well tasted, and very agreeable to those who accustom themselves to use it; instead of having any noxious quality, according to what many have experienced of the East-India insipid and costly tea, it is friendly to the human system . . . it perfectly cures a tremor in the nerves. (Adair 1775)

Naturalist William Bartram observed the plant among the Cherokee people in the late eighteenth century:

> Here I observed a little grove of the Cassine yapon, which was the only place where I had seen it grow in Cherokee country; the Indians call it the beloved tree, and are very careful to keep it pruned and cultivated: they drink a very strong infusion of the leaves, buds, and tender branches of this plant, which is so celebrated, indeed venerated by the Creeks and all of the southern maritime nations of Indians. (Bartram 1791; 1955)

Another description of the process of brewing cassina tea comes from the account of Jonathan Dickinson, who observed it in 1696 while a captive of the southeastern Florida group known as Ais. Although the Ais were not Calusa, the Calusa may have brewed their cassina tea in a similar way:

> In one part of the house where the fire was kept, was an Indian man, having a pot on the fire wherein he was making a drink of the leaves of a shrub (which we understood afterwards by the Spaniard, is called cassena), boiling the said leaves, after they had parched them in a pot; then with a gourd having a long neck and at the top of it a small hole which the top of one's finger could cover, and at the side of it a round hole of two inches diameter, they take the liquor out of the pot and put it in a deep round bowl, which being almost filled containeth nigh three gallons. With this gourd they brew the liquor and make it froth very much. It looketh of a deep brown color. . . . This drink when made, and cooled to sup, was in a conch-shell, first carried to the Caseekey, who threw part of it on the ground, and the rest he drank up, and then would make a loud He-m; and afterwards the cup passed to the rest of the Caseekey's associates. (Dickinson 1985)

ⓑⓑⓑⓑⓑⓑ

11

Calusa Architecture and Engineering

There are no standing remains of any Calusa houses or other buildings. Archaeologists have uncovered hundreds of *postmolds* (stains in the soil that mark the location of former wooden posts), but very little has yet been determined about building forms and sizes from information gathered so far. Historical documents say that south Florida Indians used fronds of the cabbage palm to make thatched roofs and sometimes walls. Today in south Florida the Seminole and Miccosukee people still use tight, waterproof palm thatch to roof their *chickees* (traditional buildings), as do many other cultures throughout the tropics worldwide.

In 1566 the Calusa leader's house (possibly also a council house, where leaders held meetings) in southwest Florida was large enough for 2,000 to stand within "without being very crowded" (Solís de Merás 1964) (figure 11.1). This could suggest either a circular building some 90 feet in diameter or perhaps a square structure about 82 feet on a side. To get some perspective on this distance, an American football field is 160 feet across, so the Calusa leader's house would have been about half the width of a football field and would have reached from the goal line almost to the 30-yard line.

We know that the Calusa structure had windows, separate rooms, and a platform on which the leader sat when he received visitors:

> 2,000 men might gather [in the cacique's house] without being very crowded ... [Governor Menéndez de Avilés] entered the cacique's house alone, with about 20 gentlemen, and stood where there were some large windows, through which he could see his men: the cacique was in a large room, alone on a [raised] seat with a great show of authority, and with an Indian woman, also seated, a little apart from him ... and there were about 500 principal Indian men and 500 Indian women: the men were near him, and the women near her, below them. (Solís de Merás 1964)

In a more recent (1696) account from southeast Florida, Jonathan Dickinson described an Ais leader's house, which may also have served as a community structure:

Figure 11.1. Artist's conception of the Calusa leader's house, in which 2,000 people could gather. (Drawing by Merald Clark.)

The Casseekey's house was about forty foot long and twenty-five foot wide, covered with palmetto leaves both top and sides. There was a range of cabins, or a barbeque on one side and two ends. At the entering on one side of the house a passage was made of benches on each side leading to the cabins. On these benches sat the chief Indians, and at the upper end of the cabin was the Casseekey seated. (Dickinson 1985)

In this context, the word "barbeque" means a wooden lattice serving as a bench or platform, from the Taino Indian word *barbacoa*. If the Ais chief's house was 40 by 25 feet, this would be 1,000 square feet (93 square meters), room for at most 300 persons if one estimates that 20 percent of the interior area was taken up by furniture, containers, hearths, and tools.

Some Calusa rituals were performed in a separate temple building, with benches, an altar or central mound, and masks covering the walls. According to Franciscan missionaries, in 1697 the temple in the Calusa leader's village was a "very tall and wide house with its door and . . . in the middle a hillock or very high flat-topped mound, and on top of it a sort of room [made] of mats with seats all closed" (Hann 1991). This sounds as though there was a mound with a structure on top of it within a larger structure.

In Dickinson's 1696 account of southeast coastal Florida, the Ais people lived in round huts with poles tied together at the top, covered with thatch. The houses stood on "hills of oyster shells," what archaeologists would probably call shell midden ridges or shell mounds today. Finally, some south Flor-

The Calusa and Their Legacy

ida coastal people lived in small houses built on pilings out over the water, as was observed in the seventeenth century by César de Rochefort: "The [people], beyond the Bays of Carlos and Tortugues, . . . lodge themselves for the most part at the entrance of the sea, in huts built on piles or pillars" (Cushing 1897).

Calusa Canals

Canals served as highways for the Calusa and their neighbors and made travel efficient (figure 11.3). They connected communities and provided protected pathways for trade, tribute, and information. These well-engineered arteries were dug by hand. Some measured thirty feet wide by six feet deep. A century ago remnants of these great canals were still readily visible, as Frank Cushing reported about the Mound Key canals:

Figure 11.2. A contemporary Kuikuru house, about sixty-five feet long, under construction in the Xingu Basin, Brazil, 1993. (Photo by Michael Heckenberger.)

ⓖⓖⓖⓖⓖⓖ

Contemporary Equivalents of Calusa Housing?

Most of us do not usually encounter enormous buildings made of wood and thatch, but in fact this kind of housing is still in use today. For example, among the Kuikuru, a fishing and agricultural society in the Xingu Basin area of Brazil, houses used for communal gatherings can measure over fifty feet long (figure 11.2).

ⓖⓖⓖⓖⓖⓖ

Mound Key... consisted of a long series of enormous elevations crowned by imposing mounds.... They were interspersed with deep inner courts, and widely surrounded with enclosures that were threaded by broad, far-reaching canals. (Cushing 1897) (figure 11.4)

About the Pine Island canal observers wrote:

The landward canal... was uniformly about thirty feet wide, and though of course now much filled, ... it still maintained an even depth of between five and six feet. (Cushing 1897)

Straight across the island ... there runs a canal or ditch which passes two ponds and another mound in the center of the island.... it shortened the distance to Matlacha Channel fully 10 miles for canoes. (M. H. Simons 1884) (figure 11.5)

Digging such canals could not have been easy. Imagine first clearing a path through mangrove and pine forests then digging and removing thousands of basketfuls of earth by hand, using only tools made of shell and wood. The canals were dug carefully and were deep and straight. This suggests good planning and effective leadership. The coordinated labor of scores of people would have been required to build and maintain these waterways.

Figure 11.3. Artist's conception of a canal leading into a Calusa village. (Drawing by Merald Clark.)

Calusa Earthworks

The Calusa made good use of their trash piles, or middens. Sometimes they used old midden material to build their mounds higher; and sometimes, as for burial of the dead, they used pure sand gathered especially for that purpose.

The earthworks of southwest Florida range from simple middens to large multiple mound complexes with unusual earthwork features. Before about

Figure 11.4. Perspective drawing of Key Marco topography, including canals and mounds. (1896 newspaper engraving, courtesy of Special Collections, University of Florida Libraries.)

Figure 11.5. The Pineland Site Complex, viewed from the air. Note remnants of the Calusa canal, still visible today. (Photo by William Marquardt.)

Figure 11.6. Brown's Mound at the Pineland Site Complex stands more than thirty feet tall. The gazebo on top is a modern addition. (Photo by Merald Clark.)

A.D. 500, the Calusa settlements in Charlotte Harbor were spread out rather than built up, and middens seem to have accumulated with no particular plan that we can perceive. Between A.D. 500 and 1000, however, people began to heap up sand and shells to make ridges and mounds (figure 11.6). Calusa villages often featured high mounds, shell ridges, canals, and broad, flat plazas. Some of the larger villages have similar town plans, often with twin mounds divided by a central canal (figure 11.7).

The Calusa probably built houses on high places for a number of reasons, perhaps including better protection from storm surges, flying insects, or human enemies. There is another important element to mound-building, too—prestige. Height often indicates power, authority, or wealth. Even in our own society, we recognize the prestige of "the house on the hill," and big businesses try to impress us with the height of their buildings.

The Anatomy of Middens and Mounds

The contents of Calusa middens and mounds enlighten us about people's diet, customs, and environment. Because middens and mounds build up and out through time, archaeologists can infer changes by digging carefully and studying their finds in detail.

Learning about changes from things found layered in the ground can be complicated, because numerous activities—from tree roots to burrowing animals to erosion to people digging pits—can disturb the various deposits, scrambling or even removing pieces of the puzzle. But the main idea that archaeologists use to interpret a site is pretty simple: the law of superposition.

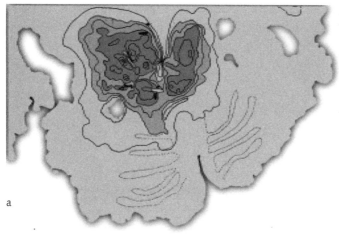

a

Figure 11.7. Topographic maps of three village sites show similar town plans with mounds and canals: (a) Big Mound Key; (b) Mound Key; (c) Pineland Site Complex. (Drawings by Merald Clark.)

b

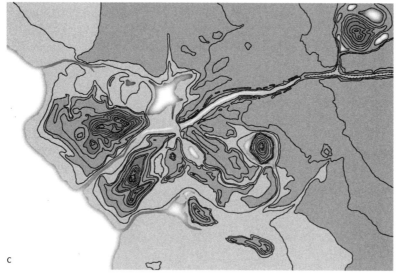

c

This means that, all other things being equal, things near the surface were deposited more recently than things found deeper. As archaeologists dig, it is as though they are reading a book backward, because they encounter the end of the story first and gradually work their way back to its beginning (figure 11.9).

Figure 11.8. Artist's conception of activities at the Pineland Site Complex. (Drawing by Bill Celander.)

ⓑⓑⓑⓑⓑⓑ

The Pineland Site Complex—Gateway to the Calusa Domain

Pineland was an important Calusa town, occupied for over 1,500 years beginning in about A.D. 50. It was located on the west coast of Pine Island, on the estuary of Charlotte Harbor/Pine Island Sound. Given its prominence, architectural complexity, and location at the entrance to the Pine Island Canal, Pineland may have been an early capital of the Calusa domain (figure 11.8). Frank Hamilton Cushing described the Pineland Site Complex, "This place—shell heaps, canals, central lagoon and all—was on a scale so vast that I could scarcely believe it to have been artificial, wholly the work of human hands" (Cushing 1897).

ⓑⓑⓑⓑⓑⓑ

Figure 11.9. A profile (section view) of an archaeological excavation at Pineland. (Photo by William Marquardt.)

For Everything, There Is a Season

Middens contain a wealth of information about people, their surroundings, and how they lived. To take just one example, animal and plant remains from middens can reveal the season in which people harvested their food. These remains tell us if people lived in a place year-round or—like many modern Floridians—for just part of the year. Archaeologists can tell the seasons when people were living at a place by the presence or the size of certain plant and animal remains. Here are a few examples.

The estuary is a nursery for many fish. Some fish spend their early life in the estuary during spring and leave later in the year for deeper water when grown. By measuring the atlas vertebrae of pinfish (*Lagodon rhomboides*) and the spines of hardhead catfish (*Arius felis*), we can tell how large the animals were. In spring most of the pinfish and catfish in the estuary are small. These fish grow larger with time, and later in the year there are greater numbers of adults.

Impressed odostomes (*Boonea impressa*) are tiny snails that are parasites on oysters. They grow larger during their year-long life. When they are found on oysters, their size tells us the season when the oysters were harvested.

A cross-section of a quahog clam (*Mercenaria campechiensis*) shell can tell us when the clam was harvested. In southwest Florida, the wide white bands form in spring when the clam grows rapidly. The narrow gray bands are from slow growth during summer, fall, and winter.

Seeds come from fruits that ripen at different times of year. For example, papaya (*Carica papaya*) ripens in July–October; hog plums (*Ximenia americana*) in March–May; mastic (*Mastichodendron foetidissimum*) in March–August; saw palmetto (*Serenoa repens*) in September–November.

Some migratory birds, such as certain ducks (Anatidae family), spend only the winter in southwest Florida; so if we find their bones, then the site must have been occupied in winter.

๑๑๑๑๑๑๑

ⓑⓑⓑⓑⓑⓑ

12

The Calusa Legacy

The Calusa and their neighbors left behind a material record of their long-standing and accomplished cultures (figure 12.1). These objects give us a window into their world, which was politically, socially, and spiritually elaborate. It is tempting to view items of Calusa manufacture in terms of what we know about them from the Spanish accounts. But the words and perceptions of the Spaniards are not those of the Calusa. Try as we might, we may never comprehend the purpose and significance of these items. Even so,

Figure 12.1. A carved and painted wooden mask from the Key Marco site. (Painting by Wells Sawyer, 1896; courtesy of Smithsonian Institution, National Anthropological Archives.)

as Seminole Mary Frances Johns said, "We've lost the meanings of these things, but even if we admire them simply as works of art, we can appreciate their makers" (Consultants 1995). With this aim in mind—appreciating the makers—we now offer a sampling of south Florida artifacts made by the Calusa and their neighbors.

Master Woodworkers

Wood was the medium of Calusa expression. It played a role in every facet of life—from canoes to containers, tools to masks, and weaponry to ornaments (figure 12.2). Excellence in woodworking is a hallmark of Calusa culture.

Figure 12.2. A carved wooden standard, Key Marco site. (Painting by Wells Sawyer, 1896; courtesy of Smithsonian Institution, National Anthropological Archives.)

Figure 12.3. This fragment of a deer-bone pin was found at the Pineland site and is 1,100 years old. The bird image was probably carved with a shark-tooth knife and may represent a merganser. (Photo by Pat Payne.)

Many of the unusual objects mentioned in this chapter were recovered from three south Florida sites with "wet" conditions that preserved wood and other organic materials.

Carved Bone and Shell

The Calusa and their neighbors also applied their talents to creative work with bone and shell. The skill and artistic sensibility of the ancient craftpersons are illustrated by a bone carved in the likeness of a pelican, an incised turtle-shell rectangle showing two leaping dolphins (both found at Key Marco), and a small fragment of a bone pin carved in the image of a duck (from Pineland) (figure 12.3). They used shell to make beads, gorgets, and pendants as well as a great variety of utilitarian items such as drinking vessels, net mesh gauges, net weights, and fishing sinkers.

Florida Wet Sites

Florida's wetlands contain many well-preserved archaeological sites. These wet sites preserve materials rarely recovered from dry-land archaeological sites because the bacteria that cause decay of organic materials cannot survive in low-oxygen wetland environments.

Conserving Wet-Site Objects

Objects from wet sites must be specially treated to prevent their deterioration. The transition from a wet environment to a dry one can cause cracking, warping, and instant decay, as Frank Cushing learned at Key Marco in 1896 (plate 39).

> Some of the things could be preserved by very slow drying, but it soon became evident that by far the greater number of them could not be kept intact. They warped, shrunk, split, and even checked across the grain, or else were utterly disintegrated on being exposed to the light and air. Fully twenty-five percent of these ancient articles in wood and other vegetal material were destroyed in the search; and of those found and removed, not more than one half retained their original forms unaltered for more than a few days. Unique to archaeology as these things were, it was distressing to feel that even by merely exposing and inspecting them, we were dooming so many of them to destruction. (Cushing 1897)

Figure 12.4. A carved and painted deer figurehead being excavated at Key Marco site, 1896. (Courtesy of Smithsonian Institution, National Anthropological Archives.)

The Calusa and Their Legacy

Cushing tried everything he could think of to preserve the Key Marco artifacts, but many were severely damaged or lost completely. Today professional *conservators* use more advanced methods to prevent the decay of wet-site objects. For example, conservators immerse some waterlogged objects in liquid chemical mixtures that gradually replace the water in the wood. This stabilizes the decaying wood cells, which would otherwise collapse as the water evaporates. Other materials, especially cloth, fibers, leather, and some woods, respond well to freeze-drying. Conservators first soak the object in a liquid chemical mixture to replace much of the water and then freeze-dry it to remove any residual water.

We now turn to a discussion of some of the artifacts that have been recovered from three important wet sites: Key Marco, Pineland, and Fort Center.

Key Marco

Perhaps the best-known archaeological site in south Florida is Key Marco, on Marco Island in present-day Collier County. Artifacts from Key Marco, excavated by Frank Cushing in 1896, are recognized worldwide as remarkable examples of Native American artistic achievement (figure 12.4). It is unparalleled in diversity of items and quality of organic preservation. Among the wooden items recovered were tools, containers, pestles, arrows, weapons, canoe paddles, tool handles, several extraordinary carved and painted masks and figureheads, and a famous wooden feline figurine six inches high. Netting made of palm fiber was found with wooden float pegs and shell weights still attached. Marine shells were used for line sinkers, net gauges, knives, woodworking tools, and hammers. Points, pins, and fishing gear were made from deer bones. Sharks' teeth served as cutting and engraving tools, antler as knife handles and adze sockets, and turtle carapace as net gauges.

Cushing's enthusiasm is evident in his written account:

> After the first day's work . . . I was left no longer in doubt as to the unique outcome of our excavations, . . . for relics . . . of new and . . . interesting varieties began at once to be found, and continued to be found increasingly as we went on day after day, throughout the entire five weeks of our work in this one little place. (Cushing 1897) (figure 12.5)

Expedition artist Wells Sawyer wrote, "Squatting on their knees in the slime, with hands and arms covered with mud, these men worked day after day, bringing forth treasures which, if seen now as we saw them, would command the attention of every student of American archaeology" (Gilliland 1989) (figure 12.6).

Figure 12.5. Frank Cushing on his boat the *Silver Spray*, during excavations at Key Marco in 1896. (Painting by Wells Sawyer, courtesy of Family of Marion S. Gilliland in her memory; photo by Jeff Gage.)

Figure 12.6. Excavators working at the Key Marco site, 1896. (Painting by Wells Sawyer, courtesy of Family of Marion S. Gilliland in her memory; photo by Jeff Gage.)

Woodpecker Plaque

This ivory-billed woodpecker, now an extinct species, was painted more than 1,200 years ago by the Indian people who lived on Marco Island (plate 40). Many native southeastern North American peoples honored woodpeckers for their roles in origin stories and as symbols of war. The circles near the bird's beak, once colored blue, white, and red, may represent speech or a call—or perhaps something altogether different.

Seminole Mary Frances Johns mused:

> It reminds me of the beadspitter. There used to be a healing art called bead spitting. And it was a way to predict the future, tell the outcome of a disease, a way of prognosticating. It was a matter of having four of four colors of beads. You put them in your mouth and then as you spit them, the position in which they came out, order and color and things like that, determined the outcome of the situation you were working with. (Consultants 1995)

Masks and Figureheads

People carved masks and figureheads throughout south Florida. Among the best-known are the items excavated by Frank Cushing at Key Marco (plates 41 and 42):

> To me, the remains that were most significant of all discovered by us in the depths of the muck were the carved and painted wooden masks and animal figureheads. The masks were exceptionally well modeled, usually in realistic representation of human features, and were life-size; hollowed to fit the face, and provided at either side, both above and below, with string-holes for attachment thereto. Some of them were also bored at intervals along the top, for the insertion of feathers or other ornaments, and others were accompanied by thick, gleaming white conchshell eyes. . . . Of these masks we found fourteen or fifteen fairly well-preserved specimens, besides numerous others, which were so decayed that, although not lost to study, they could not be recovered. (Cushing 1897)

Painted Box Sides

These pieces of wood once formed the sides of a box (figure 12.7). The reptile design painted on the inside of the box looks like an alligator, although a now-faded horn suggests a more unusual creature, possibly similar to the horned serpent of later Seminole Indian stories.

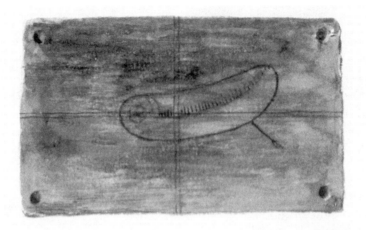

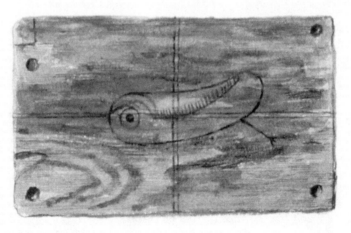

Figure 12.7. Box sides with painted images from Key Marco, including a reptile (center) and two unidentified forms. (Painting by Wells Sawyer, 1896; courtesy of Smithsonian Institution, National Anthropological Archives.)

Mary Frances Johns related, "The horned serpent took the boy back to his home from another land. In the process of traveling on the serpent's back, he had been filing on one of the horns the whole time, and he had it filed almost down to where it would be easy to break off and as he jumped off he pulled on that horn and it came off in his hand and he took off for shore. It became a hunting talisman of great power" (Consultants 1995).

Other Items

Plate 43 shows a variety of other items from Key Marco. Although not as charismatic as painted masks, these objects provide insight into daily life in early south Florida.

Pineland

The Pineland Site Complex is located on Pine Island near Fort Myers, Florida. Excavations there in 1992 yielded perishables preserved as well as those of Key Marco, including not only cordage and wood but uncharred squash, papaya, and chile pepper seeds almost 2,000 years old (figure 12.8). The papaya seeds are the only ones found in any North American archaeological context, and the chile peppers are the only ones known east of the Mississippi River. Pineland's mounds (over 30 feet tall) and canal (30 feet wide) suggest its importance to Calusa politics and trade. The Pineland site is the subject of continuing excavations and holds great potential for further discoveries. (You can visit the Pineland site—see "Randell Research Center at Pineland" in the "Places to Visit" section at the end of this book.)

Waterbird Figure

A carved cypress figure, about 1,100 years old, represents the head and upper beak of a waterbird, probably a crane (figure 12.9). In its original form the bird may have been painted and decorated. The lower beak is missing but would have been connected to the head by string. The Calusa may have used the bird in dramatic performances, opening and closing the bird's beak by pulling the string (figure 12.10). A similar tradition is known among the Kwakiutl and other Indian people of the Northwest Coast of North America, and bird headdresses are shown in engraved shells found in sites of the Late Mississippian period (about A.D. 1000–1400) in the southeastern United States.

Figure 12.8. Excavations in wet deposits at the Pineland site, 1992. (Photo by Karen Walker.)

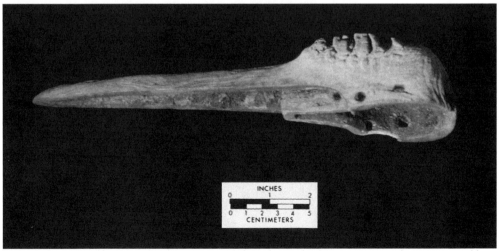

Figure 12.9. Carving of a crane's head (cypress wood) from the Pineland site, approximately 1,100 years old. (Photo by John Knaub.)

Figure 12.10. Artist's sketches of possible uses of the crane figurehead. (Illustration by Merald Clark.)

Figure 12.11. A wooden eagle carving from Fort Center, about 1,500 to 1,800 years old. (Photo by Roy Craven, courtesy of Barbara Purdy.)

The bird head reminded Seminole Mary Frances Johns of the legend of the wood stork, here called a wood ibis:

> When the world was being created by the One Above, the sun was really bright and he lighted up the area where he was, and the creatures that were in his presence rejoiced wherever he went. But those that didn't have him, they were freezing to death. So somebody suggested that the sunshine could be put up in the sky to warm everybody. But they didn't quite know how to get him up there, because the sun was really hot, he was like a volcano, so he was real hard to handle. The one that did it was the wood ibis. He was able to fly to the sky and put him in his house up there. So we had sunlight for everybody. That is how the wood ibis lost the feathers off of his head because he got burned down to the chest. (Consultants 1995)

Fort Center

The village archaeologists call Fort Center is located inland on the western side of Lake Okeechobee. Large mounds and other earthworks mark the site, which was occupied for 2,000 years.

Archaeologists refer to the people who lived in this area during Calusa times as the "Belle Glade" culture. Belle Glade people traveled west to the Gulf coast by canoe through a series of canals and natural drainages in order to visit, trade with, and pay tribute to the Calusa. Like other peoples of south Florida, they were once part of the Calusa domain.

Woodcarvings

At Fort Center, archaeologists discovered woodcarvings preserved for more than 1,500 years in the muck of a pond. Most of the carvings depict animals perched on top of posts that could have been anchored into the ground or the pond bottom (figure 12.11). These posts may have been markers for a burial platform because bundled burials were also found in the pond. Although years of decay have obscured the finely carved details, some of the animal forms are still recognizable. Several wooden human figurines have also been found in the Lake Okeechobee area, not far from Fort Center (plate 44).

New Materials, Ancient Designs

Spaniards took precious metals such as silver and gold from Indian people in northern South America and sent them to Spain. Some of the ships transporting the gold and silver wrecked on Florida's coast. South Florida Indian people fashioned traditional ornaments from metals they recovered from shipwrecks. Although the medium was new, the objects were still in keeping with traditional designs (plate 45).

Plate 1. A part of the Charlotte Harbor Estuarine System, seen from the air. (Photo by Corbett Torrence.)

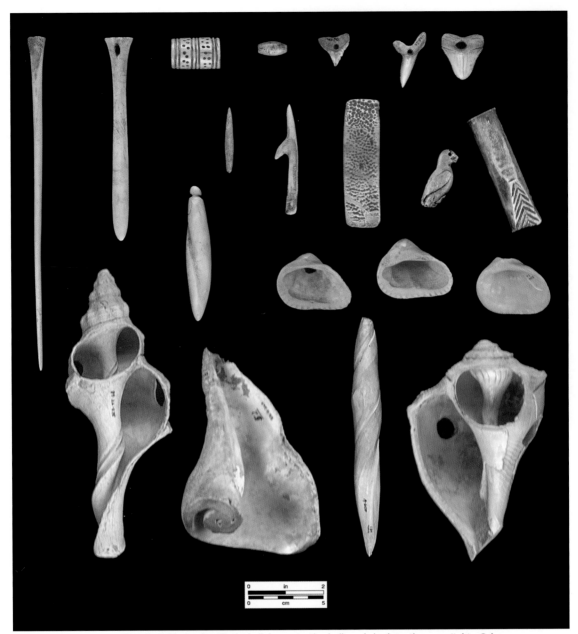

Plate 2. Artifacts of mollusk shell, bone, turtle shell, and shark teeth were vital to Calusa daily life (left to right, top to bottom): deer-bone pin, deer-bone net shuttle, bone beads (2), perforated shark teeth (3), deer-bone point, deer-bone barb for composite fish hook, turtle-bone net-mesh gauge, bone carved into bird image, antler socket, whelk-shell sinker, arc-shell net weights (3), conch-shell hammer, whelk-shell grinder/pulverizer, whelk-shell perforator, whelk-shell cutting-edged tool. (Photos by Jeff Gage, graphic by Pat Payne.)

Plate 3. The estuary at Big Jim Creek, Charlotte Harbor. (Photo by Robert Repenning, courtesy of Florida Department of Environmental Protection.)

Plate 4. Various algae (both red and green) in the Charlotte Harbor estuary. (Photo by David Harlos.)

Plate 5. Fiddler crabs (*Uca* sp.) scurry across a mudflat at low tide. Crabs with one big claw are males. (Photo by Darcie MacMahon.)

Plate 6. The shelly tubes of decorator worms (*Diopatra cuprea*) exposed on a mudflat at low tide. (Photo by Dorr Dennis.)

Plate 7. A brittle star (*Ophiolepus elegans*) blends in well with the muddy bottom. (Photo by Jeff Gage.)

Plate 8. An oyster bar, exposed at low tide. (Photo by Karen Walker.)

Plate 9. At low tide, a crown conch (*Melongena corona*) moves across a shelly mudflat on its black and white foot. (Photo by Dorr Dennis.)

Plate 10. Roseate spoonbills (*Ajaia ajaja*) near shore in a mangrove estuary. (Photo by Robert Repenning, courtesy of Florida Department of Environmental Protection.)

Plate 11. Sea grasses host other plants and animals on their blades. (Photo courtesy of South Florida Water Management District.)

Plate 12. Pink shrimp (*Farfantepenaeus duorarum*) are common in Florida's estuaries and are a popular food. (Photo by David Harlos.)

Plate 13. A bay scallop (*Argopecten irradians*) filters food from the water. The eyes along the edge of the shell detect moving shadows and cause the shell to snap shut. (Photo by Jay Leverone, courtesy of Tampa Bay Estuary Program.)

Plate 14. An elongated lettuce sea slug (*Elysia crispata*) seen from the underside. Its green color is due to chloroplasts from algae that it eats. The chloroplasts continue to live and photosynthesize in the animal's tissues, producing sugars that are good for the animal's nutrition. (Photo by Jeff Gage.)

Plate 15. A brown spiny sea star (*Echinaster spinulosus*) crawls on tube feet across a rock. (Photo by David Harlos.)

Plate 16. Beachcombers think of sand dollars (*Mellita quinquiesperforata*) as white; but the live animal, covered with tiny spines, is gray-brown to blend in with its environment. (Photo by Jeff Gage.)

Plate 17. Sea grasses provide surfaces on which algae and various animals live. (Photo by Gary Lytton, courtesy of Rookery Bay National Estuarine Research Reserve.)

Plate 18. An eroded sponge (*Haliclona loosanoffi*) growing among oysters. (Photo by Karen Walker.)

Plate 19. Sea whips (*Leptogorgia virgulata*) are colonial animals and also host other animal residents and visitors. (Photo by Jeff Gage.)

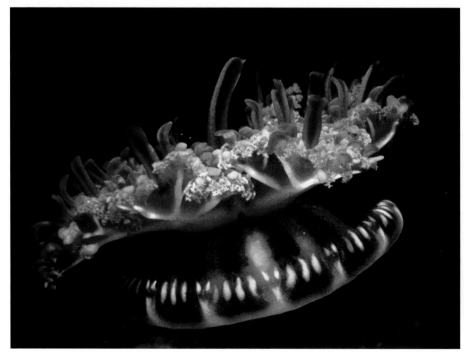

Plate 20. An up-side-down jellyfish (*Cassiopeia xamacha-na*) prepares to rest on the estuary bottom. (Photo by Anne DuPont.)

Plate 21. Luminous rows of cilia on one of the comb jellies from Florida (*Beroe ovata* Harris). (Photo by Carmen Merriam, courtesy of Mote Marine Laboratory.)

Plate 22. A Gulf pipefish (*Sygnathus scovelli*) camouflaged among sea grasses. (Photo by David Harlos.)

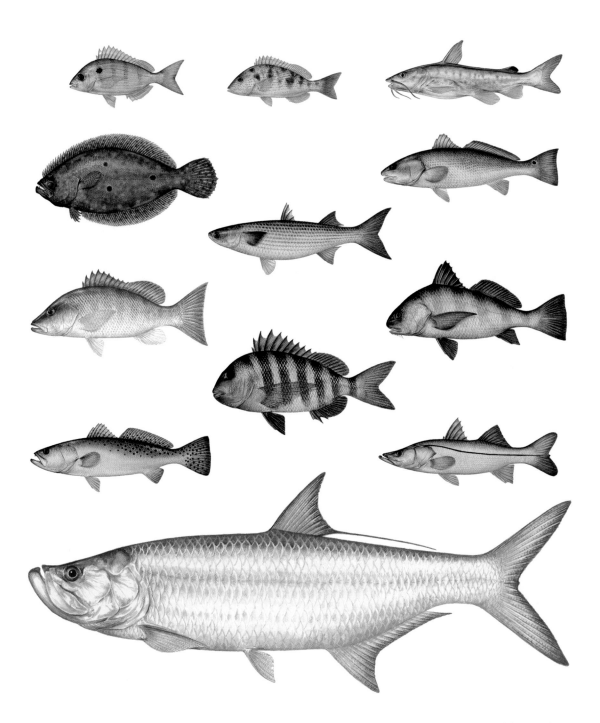

Plate 23. Examples of fish that depend on a healthy estuary for survival (left to right, top to bottom): pinfish (*Lagodon rhomboides*); pigfish (*Orthopristis chrysoptera*); hardhead catfish (*Arius felis*); Gulf flounder (*Paralichthys albigutta*); juvenile redfish (*Sciaenops ocellatus*); mullet (*Mugil* sp.); mangrove snapper (*Lutjanus griseus*); black drum (*Pogonias cromis*); sheepshead (*Archosargus probatocephalus*); spotted seatrout (*Cynoscion nebulosus*); snook (*Centropomus undecimalis*); tarpon (*Megalops atlanticus*). (Illustrations by Diane Peebles, courtesy of Florida Fish and Wildlife Conservation Commission; graphic by Pat Payne.)

Plate 24. A juvenile loggerhead sea turtle (*Caretta caretta*) glides through the water. (Photo by Don DeMaria.)

Plate 25. Mangrove roots protect fish and other animals from predators. (Photo by Janet Ley.)

Plate 26. A colony of glass tunicates (*Ecteinascidia turbinata*). (Photo by David Harlos.)

Plate 27. A community of pale anemones (*Aiptasia pallida*). (Photo by Jeff Gage.)

Plate 28. A mangrove crab (*Aratus pisonii*) camouflaged on mangrove bark. (Photo by Robert Repenning, courtesy of Florida Department of Environmental Protection.)

Plate 29. A mangrove water snake (*Nerodia fasciata compressicauda*). (Photo by Richard D. Bartlett.)

Plate 30. A male mangrove skipper (*Phocides pigmalion okeechobee*). (Photo by Elton Woodbury, courtesy of Association for Tropical Lepidoptera.)

Plate 31. Mangrove periwinkles (*Littoraria angulifera*) mating on a red mangrove leaf. (Photo by William Marquardt.)

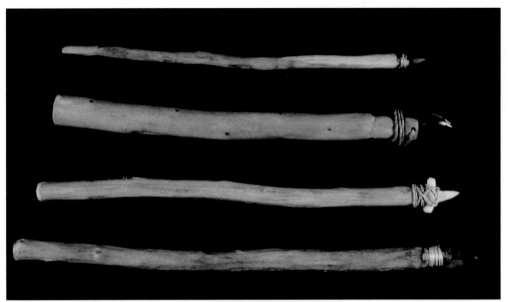

Plate 32. Shark-tooth knives and drills. (Reproductions and photo by Robin Brown.)

Plate 33. A variety of Calusa shell tools (left to right, top to bottom): conch-shell sinker, whelk-shell hammer, clam-shell knife/scraper, whelk-shell cup, whelk-shell cutting-edged tool, whelk-shell sinker. (Photos by Jeff Gage, graphic by Pat Payne.)

Plate 40. Woodpecker plaque, Key Marco site, Collier County, cypress wood with natural pigments, ca. A.D. 800. (Photo by John Knaub.)

Plate 41. Wooden carvings from Key Marco (counterclockwise from top): wolf, falcon, alligator, panther. (First three are paintings by Wells Sawyer, courtesy of National Anthropological Archives, Smithsonian Institution; panther photo courtesy of Department of Anthropology, Smithsonian Institution, catalogue #240915; graphic by Pat Payne.)

Plate 42. Masks from the Key Marco site. (Paintings by Wells Sawyer, 1896; courtesy of Smithsonian Institution, National Anthropological Archives; graphic by Pat Payne.)

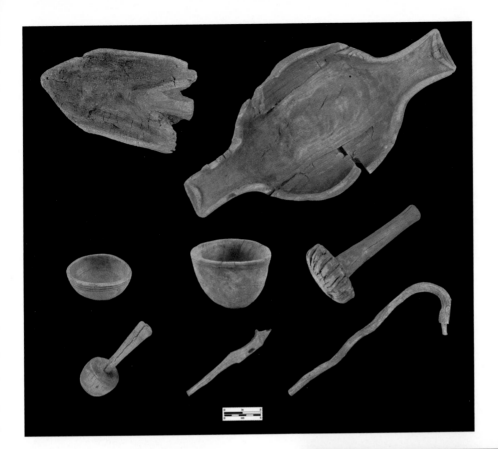

Plate 43. Wooden artifacts from Key Marco (top to bottom, left to right): leaf-shaped tray/bowl; tray with carved handles; bowls (2); pestle; mallet; tool handle; carved wooden socketed handle. (Photos by Jeff Gage, graphic by Pat Payne.)

Plate 44. Carved wooden human figurines from south Florida: (left) figurine, lignum vitae wood, date unknown, Lake Okeechobee; (right) figurine, date unknown, Belle Glade, Palm Beach County. (Photos by Robert Leavy, courtesy of Smithsonian Institution, National Museum of Natural History.)

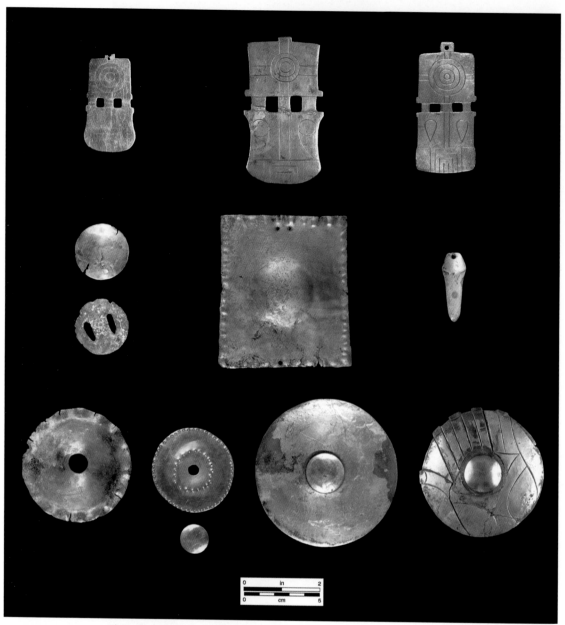

Plate 45. Ornaments of metal from post-contact south Florida, A.D. 1550–1650 (left to right, top to bottom): incised gold tablet; incised silver tablets (2); gold ornament with lead backing; embossed silver gorget; silver shark-tooth pendant; cone-shaped copper disk; embossed gold disk and gold button; embossed silver disk and silver button; engraved silver disk and gold button. Gold tablet, upper left, is from the Pineland Site Complex; all other objects are from Fort Center. (Photos by Jeff Gage, graphic by Pat Payne.)

Plate 46. Beads, ceramics, and ceramic doll's leg from eighteenth and early nineteenth century Cuban fishing village on Useppa Island. (Photos by Scott Mitchell and Pat Payne; graphic by Pat Payne.)

Plate 47. Artifacts from Oven Hill site (top to bottom, left to right): brushed pots (2); metal pail; bottle fragment; ceramic fragment. (Photos by Jeff Gage, graphic by Pat Payne.)

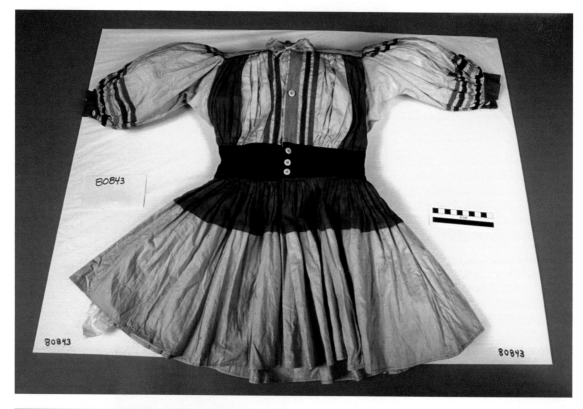

Plate 48. Boy's big shirt, maker unknown, about 1910. (Photo by Jeff Gage.)

Plate 49. Martha Jones sewing patchwork, Brighton Reservation, 2000. (Photo by Darcie MacMahon.)

Plate 50. Seminole boys at a costume competition. (Courtesy of Seminole Communications, Seminole Tribe of Florida.)

Plate 51. Seminole dolls: (left) palmetto-fiber cowboy doll (made by Mable Osceola, Hollywood, 2000); (top) palmetto fiber dolls, male and female (from Musa Isles Village, 1930–31); (bottom) carved wooded dolls, male and female (collected from Deaconess Bedell, Tamiami Trail, 1950). (Photos by Jeff Gage, graphic by Pat Payne.)

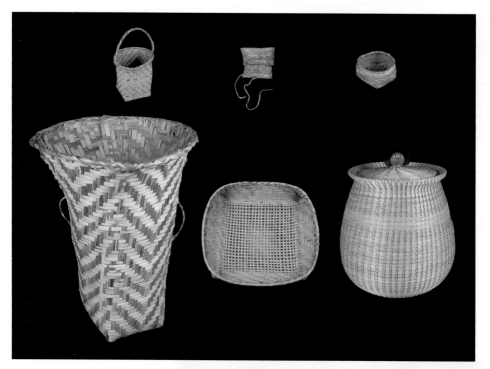

Plate 52. Seminole baskets (left to right, top to bottom): palmetto "berry basket" (from Bert Lasher's camp, Miami, 1943); palmetto medicine basket (1930s to 1950s); split cane basket (1841–42); palmetto burden basket (made by Adah Tiger, Dania Reservation, 1942); palmetto sifter basket (from Josie Billie's camp, Tamiami Trail, 1940s to 1950s); coiled sweet-grass basket with doll lid (made by Agnes Billie Cypress [basket] and Lucy Johns [lid], Immokalee, 1997). (Photos by Jeff Gage, graphic by Pat Payne.)

Plate 53. Mary Frances Johns makes a coiled pine-needle basket, with sweetgrass basket in fore-ground, 2000. (Photo by Darcie MacMahon.)

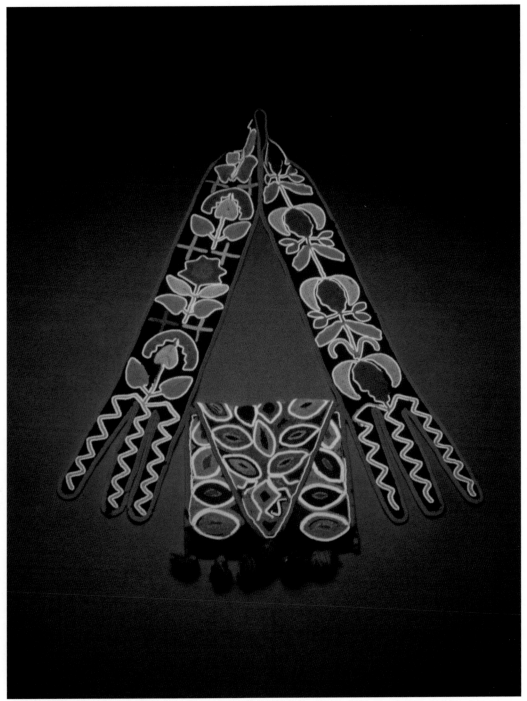

Plate 54. Man's beaded shoulder bag from the early 1800s. (Photo by Florida Museum of Natural History.)

Plate 55. Fingerwoven garters. (Photo by Jeff Gage.)

Plate 56. Five generations of women from Susie Billie's family share stories, 2000. (Photo by Darcie MacMahon.)

13

ᘰᘰᘰᘰᘰᘰ

The Calusa and the Europeans

When Juan Ponce de León encountered the Calusa Indians in southwest Florida in 1513, he was not hospitably received. The Calusa already knew that Spaniards had enslaved and murdered Caribbean Indians, because they had allowed refugees from Cuba to settle in south Florida. The Calusa continued to resist European domination for nearly 200 years, but in the early 1700s they finally lost their hold on their ancient homeland. In this chapter, we explore some of the reasons why south Florida Indian people and Europeans could not coexist in harmony and describe some of the consequences of European contact with the Florida natives.

Early Encounters

The Indian people of south Florida probably learned about Columbus's 1492 landing in the Caribbean and had firsthand knowledge of Spanish merchants or slavers by 1511. They also knew that Spanish invaders had devastated the Indian population of Cuba.

Ponce de León's three ships first landed on the east coast of Florida in the spring of 1513. By late May his ships were in southwest Florida waters. The Spanish skirted Cayo Costa, North Captiva, Captiva, and Sanibel islands to the mouth of the Caloosahatchee River at San Carlos Bay, where they decided to careen one of their vessels. Over the course of the next ten days, several parties of Indians approached in canoes, offering to trade. On June 4 another canoe arrived, carrying an Indian who understood Spanish. He may have been one of the group of Cuban refugees who had fled the Spanish conquest after 1511. This man carried a message from the Calusa leader for the Spaniards to wait for his arrival, but soon the Spaniards were attacked by warriors in twenty Calusa canoes (figure 13.1). The Calusa were repulsed, and some were killed and captured. Spaniards sent two captives to the Calusa leader with a message. The following day, as one of the vessels was sounding the depths of a port (possibly San Carlos Bay), a larger force of men in eighty

Figure 13.1.
According to first-
hand accounts,
Calusa people
resisted Ponce de
León's attempts
to land in their
territory in the
early 1500s.
(Drawing by Mer-
ald Clark.)

shielded canoes attacked the Spaniards. The skirmish lasted until dark, and both sides retreated without damage. The Spaniards remained until June 14, when they set sail southward on the way back to Puerto Rico.

Ponce de León and his associates did not return to Florida immediately. The ships of Francisco Hernández de Córdoba stopped briefly on the southwest Florida coast in 1517 and were attacked. The Spaniards killed twenty-three native people. In 1521 Ponce de León again reached southwest Florida, intending to build a settlement. His settlers were attacked, and many were wounded, including Ponce de León himself. His wound proved fatal.

Spanish encounters in western Florida continued. In 1528 the Pánfilo de Narváez expedition landed in the Tampa Bay area, well north of Charlotte Harbor, encountering many native groups during a long series of misadventures. In 1539 Hernando de Soto's complement of soldiers, horses, and pigs landed on the Florida west coast just north of Calusa territory and made its way to present-day north Florida, murdering and pillaging along the way. Certainly the Calusa learned of the expeditions of Narváez and de Soto. When some Dominican missionaries briefly visited the central Gulf coast in 1549, they encountered hostility. Shipwrecks in the 1540s and 1550s brought the Calusa Spanish goods and captives, including the boy Hernando de Escalante Fontaneda. Fontaneda lived among the Calusa for seventeen years and played a pivotal role in the encounters between Spanish governor Pedro Menéndez de Avilés and Calusa leader Caalus in 1566 and 1567.

Increased Contact

Having driven the French from St. Augustine in the fall of 1565, Menéndez turned his attention to the remainder of the peninsula. The first sustained contact between the Calusa and the Spaniards began in February 1566. As described in chapter 10, the Calusa leader Caalus met Spanish governor Menéndez in an immense house. The two leaders reached an alliance, but it did not last.

Menéndez established several forts across south Florida, including one at the Calusa capital on Mound Key. A Jesuit missionary was stationed there to try to convert the Calusa to Catholicism (figure 13.2). When relations deteriorated, Spanish soldiers killed two successive Calusa leaders and many nobles. Throughout this turbulent time, the Calusa remained true to their own spiritual beliefs. The mission of San Antón de Carlos failed and was abandoned in 1569.

Documents written as a result of the first intensive European and Calusa contact from 1566 to 1569 say that the Calusa leader's domain included at least fifty towns and that he collected tribute from many more. The Calusa were at war with the Tocobaga, who lived at present-day Tampa Bay, but the Calusa exerted control over most of the rest of south Florida. By 1612 the Calusa leader directly controlled over sixty towns, and many more paid him tribute. In 1614 the Calusa waged war against Spanish-allied Indian people at modern Tampa Bay, and the Spaniards retaliated.

So far as we now know, Spaniards did not return to southwest Florida until the late 1600s. The Calusa had apparently decided to isolate themselves from Europeans, although they still held some European captives. In 1680 Florida governor Pablo de Hita Salazar sent a Spanish soldier-interpreter with a party of Timucuan Indians to try to ransom some Spanish captives held by the Calusa. The group traveled from St. Augustine across northern Florida then down the Gulf coast toward Calusa territory. Local Indian people begged the expedition to turn back for fear that the Calusa leader would have them executed if he learned that they had allowed the Spanish expedition to pass. The Indian guides finally fled, and the expedition turned back to St. Augustine.

This account suggests that as of 1680 the Calusa not only were still in control of their traditional lands but also were avoiding the hostilities be-

Figure 13.2. Jesuit missionaries attempted unsuccessfully to convert the Calusa. (Drawing by Merald Clark.)

tween the Spanish and English that were steadily eroding Spanish control of northern Florida. Indeed, the Calusa still lived in their coastal towns as late as 1697, when Franciscan missionaries from Cuba attempted to establish another mission (figure 13.3). The Franciscans stayed only a few months, driven out when they insisted that the Calusa give up their rituals and beliefs.

The Demise of Calusa Society

War broke out in 1702 between England and the allied powers of France and Spain. The English occupied St. Augustine and attacked Spanish garrisons and outposts in the vicinity. In 1704 the English and their Creek Indian allies overwhelmed Spanish and Apalachee Indian defenses in northwestern Florida, destroying the line of Spanish missions and garrisons that stretched from St. Augustine to Tallahassee. About 1,000 Apalachee Indians were taken to Carolina to be enslaved.

One result of this destruction of Spanish settlements was that Indian people who had been displaced from their own territories began to move into the abandoned lands. Another result was that armed Uchise Creek and Yamassee Indians moved farther into the Florida peninsula, capturing south Florida Indian people for sale as slaves in the English colonies. The Creeks and Yamassees had been displaced by raiding, colonization, and wars of

Figure 13.3. This Spanish letter, written in 1692 by the bishop of Cuba to the king of Spain, supports a new mission to the Calusa. (Courtesy of Special Collections, University of Florida Libraries.)

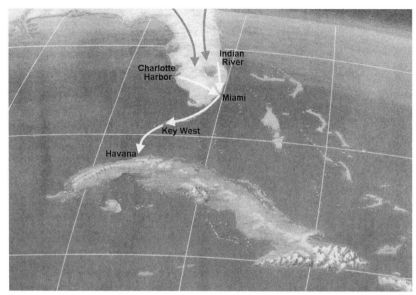

Figure 13.4. The Calusa were driven from their homeland between 1704 and 1711. (Map by John Worth.)

the English and Spanish and had become professional slavers. The English traded muskets for Indian slaves, so the Creeks and Yamassees were well armed. Having isolated themselves from the Europeans in the 1600s, the Calusa and other south Florida people had no such weapons and were no match for the invading slave hunters. Within a few years after 1704, the remaining Calusa who had not succumbed to European diseases, warfare, or enslavement had been driven from their traditional lands and waters. Some concentrated around St. Augustine, others east and south of the Everglades.

Yamassees and Creeks continued to hunt native south Florida Indian people in the Keys in attempts to enslave them for sale to the English. Among these Keys residents were the remnants of several south Florida tribes, including the Calusa. In 1711 the Calusa paramount leader led 270 Indian people to Cuba, and others followed later (figure 13.4). Some 1,700 south Florida Indian people could not go to Cuba because there was no more room on the ship. Of the 270 who went to Havana with the Spaniards, over 200 died quickly from diseases, including four of the hereditary leaders, among them the Calusa leader.

Jesuit missionaries tried to establish a mission in the Florida Keys in 1743, but the Indian people there—perhaps realizing the strategic importance of a Spanish presence in south Florida—demanded clothing, food, and rum and never seriously considered becoming Christians. The last south Florida native people left for Cuba in 1760 after a final devastating Creek raid. At the conclusion of the Seven Years' War in 1763, Florida was transferred to England in exchange for Havana. The Calusa fade from the Florida historical record at this time, although some of their descendants may survive in Cuba today.

Are There Calusa Indian People in South Florida Today?

Calusa and other south Florida Indian people served as hired hands on Cuban fishing vessels, probably as early as the late 1680s and certainly through 1760. Historical documents refer to "Spanish Indians" who lived on the southwest Florida coast in the late 1700s and early 1800s and worked there with Cuban fisherfolk. After 1760 these so-called Spanish Indians were probably the descendants of Creek, Yamassee, and other northern groups that had migrated into Florida.

Some Calusa people may have escaped enslavement and lived on in south Florida, perhaps along with the newly arrived native peoples from the north, today known as the Seminole and Miccosukee peoples. Some Seminole people have a saying that if a person is tall, he or she must be Calusa. In the 1930s Smithsonian folklorist Frances Densmore collected songs among the Seminole people that were attributed to the "Calusa." She reported, "The singer said . . . that long ago the Calusa and Seminole camped near one another and the people of each camp visited freely in the other, learning songs and joining in the dances" (Densmore 1956).

Some writers have speculated that Chakaika, a "Spanish Indian" leader in the Second Seminole War in the 1830s, had Calusa ancestry. Most historians are doubtful about such stories, because they are not based on written documents.

As intriguing as stories of remnant Calusa people are, from a practical perspective the Calusa are gone from Florida. We mean this in two senses. First, there is no specific place in Florida, including their ancient homeland in the southwestern part of the state, where one can go to meet and talk with Calusa people. Second, there are no known living speakers of the Calusa language in Florida.

From another outlook, the Calusa are still with us. As Seminole Mary Frances Johns remarked, "If we are still talking about them, then they are not really gone" (Consultants 1995). The Calusa remain with us in the remarkable earthworks, canals, and artwork that they left behind. The Calusa themselves believed that upon death their spirits passed into smaller animals or fish and then to other smaller ones when those died. From the Calusa point of view, then, their spirits can still be found in the leap of the dolphin, the flight of the pelican, and the cry of the panther.

ⓖⓖⓖⓖⓖⓖ

14

Fishing since the Calusa

Calusa society had disintegrated by the early 1700s due to European-introduced diseases, warfare, and slavery; but fishing continued. In fact, fishing technology did not change much until the advent of monofilament nets, motorized boats, and modern refrigeration in the mid twentieth century.

Cuban and Indian Fishing in Southwest Florida

In the mid 1700s Spanish fisherfolk from Cuba arrived in southwest Florida and were joined by Indian people moving into the area from present-day Georgia, Alabama, and north Florida. These Indian people traded animal skins for salt and dry goods with the Cubans on the Gulf coast. Some fished with the Cubans, and Europeans referred to these people as "Spanish Indians." Although some migrated into Florida from the north, others may have been remnants of southwest Florida coastal tribes such as the Calusa and Muspa. Even earlier, south Florida natives had traveled regularly to Havana. In the late 1600s they traded fish and ambergris (a whale secretion used in perfume) as well as fruit, hides, turtle shells, and cardinal birds. A century later, Indian people were observed in Cuba trading fish, skins, furs, honey, and bear grease for rum, coffee, sugar, and tobacco. Naturalist William Bartram observed:

> These Indians have large handsome canoes, which they form out of the trunks of Cypress trees, some of them commodious enough to accommodate twenty or thirty warriors. In these large canoes they descend the river on trading and hunting expeditions to the sea coast, neighbouring islands and keys, quite to the point of Florida, and sometimes cross the gulph, extending their navigations to the Bahama islands and even to Cuba: a crew of these adventurers had just arrived, having returned from Cuba but a few days before our arrival, with a cargo of spirituous liquors, Coffee, Sugar, and Tobacco. One of them politely presented me with a

choice piece of Tobacco, which he told me he had received from the governor of Cuba. (Bartram 1791; 1955)

By 1765 Cubans had set up seasonal fish camps, called "ranchos," along the Gulf coast, from Tampa Bay to Charlotte Harbor (figure 14.1). Working with Indian people from September through March, the fisherfolk caught mullet, redfish, grouper, pompano, and sea trout. Drying and salting preserved the fish for shipment to Cuba. They also smoked mullet and redfish roe and processed shark livers to make oil. Their ranchos consisted of palmetto-thatched huts (figure 14.2). Fishing gear included nets, containers for salt and other essentials, and drying racks and grills for processing the catch. Some fisherfolk elected to stay in southwest Florida the whole year, hunting, fishing, and cultivating gardens during the summer months.

Figure 14.1. Artist's conception of a scene at a Cuban fishing rancho, late 1700s to early 1800s, coastal southwest Florida. (Drawing by Merald Clark.)

Figure 14.2. Cuban fish-processing camps probably resembled this camp on Cayo Costa, Charlotte Harbor, about 1900. (Photo courtesy of Richard Coleman.)

William Bartram had this to say in 1774 about the Cuban fishermen he observed in present-day Charlotte Harbor:

The Spaniards of Cuba likewise trade [at] ... other sea ports on the west coast of the isthmus, in small sloops; particularly at the bay of Calos, where are excellent fishing banks and grounds; not far from which is a considerable town of the Siminoles, where they take great quantities of fish, which they salt and cure on shore, and barter with the Indians and traders for skins, furs, &c. and return with their cargoes to Cuba. (Bartram 1791; 1955)

England governed Florida from 1763 to 1783. When England gave Florida back to Spain, the Cuban fishing ranchos became more firmly established. Until the 1830s one of the largest and most successful of the ranchos was located on Useppa Island (plate 46). About twenty palmetto-thatched houses accommodated fifty to sixty residents, including both Spanish Cubans and Native Americans. For several generations, Native Americans traded with, fished with, and sometimes married Cuban fishermen. Some of the children of Cuban-Indian unions received educations and religious instruction in Cuba.

This well-established partnership between Native American and Cuban fisherfolk was not to last, however. After 1814, following the Creek War, more Indian people from present-day Georgia migrated into Florida. By this time, English-speaking Euro-Americans referred to all Florida Indian people as

"Seminoles," a word derived from the Spanish word *cimarrones*, meaning wild or untamed.

Spain ceded Florida to the United States in 1821; and in the 1830s the United States sought to force removal of all Indian people west of the Mississippi River, including the so-called Spanish Indians. Resistance to removal led to the 1835–42 Second Seminole War. This war effectively ended the long fishing partnership between Spanish Cuban and Florida Indian people along Florida's Gulf coast. Later, the Civil War hindered fishing in southwest Florida because of a Union naval blockade intended to prevent delivery of supplies to Confederate forces.

After the Civil War, Hispanic fisherfolk and traders reestablished themselves in Charlotte Harbor. One of these families was that of Tariva and Laini ("Juanita") Padilla (figure 14.3). Tariva Padilla was born in the Canary Islands but immigrated to the Florida Keys; Laini was born in Mexico. In 1876 they settled on Cayo Costa Island, joining other fishing families already in residence there. By 1879 there were four fishing villages operating in Charlotte Harbor. Some of the commercial fishing families in present-day south-

Figure 14.3. Tariva Padilla (fifth from left in photo), from Spain's Canary Islands, began a long family tradition of fishing and trading in the Charlotte Harbor area. (Photo about 1901, courtesy of Perry Padilla.)

west Florida are descended from these early Hispanic fisherfolk. By the 1890s mullet and other fish were again being caught, salted, dried, and transported to Cuba by schooner, much as they had been during the previous Spanish-Indian fishing era, ca. 1765–1835.

Technology Changes the Fishing Industry

Beginning in the 1890s, the invention of the ice plant and the arrival of railroads allowed fish to be sent to northern markets. Many fisherfolk from the Carolinas came to Florida to work in the lucrative net-fishing trade. By 1910 packing "fresh" fish in ice had replaced the salt-fish industry.

Like the Calusa, twentieth-century fisherfolk used many kinds of nets—gill nets, dip nets, cast nets, and more (figure 14.4). Fishers in the nineteenth and early twentieth centuries used nets made of cotton and flax. Monofilament nets had replaced natural fiber nets by the 1960s. Monofilament nets had advantages. It was harder for the fish to see them, and they were much

Figure 14.4. Esperanza Woodring net-fishing in 1949. (Photo by J. Charles McCullough II.)

Figure 14.5. Fisherman weaving a cast net, 1958. (Photo courtesy of Florida State Archives.)

stronger and needed less maintenance. But nets have always required a lot of work to make and maintain (figure 14.5). As life-long commercial fisherwoman Nellie Coleman put it in a 1990 interview:

> I hate hanging nets and mending nets, and, when I got out of it, I swore I'd never do it again. If you have a net, you have to keep working on it. It's like a boat and a motor. There's always something wrong with it; you have to keep working on it, no matter what kind you got. (Edic 1996)

Listening to today's senior fisherfolk reflect on the work involved in caring for their flax and cotton fishing nets gives us a perspective on Indian fishing. Just as early twentieth century fishers had to tar and lime their nets and hang them out to dry, the Calusa must have done similar work on their palm-fiber nets. As Ms. Coleman says, "If you have a net, you have to keep working on it" (figure 14.6).

Figure 14.6. Net-mending party at Gasparilla Village, about 1920. (Photo courtesy of Eunice Albritton.)

𝕺𝕺𝕺𝕺𝕺𝕺

Modern Net-Fishing Reflections

In those days, everybody used cotton nets. Natural fibers, flax or cotton. Had to spread those nets cause if you didn't spread them they'd rot. Had to lime them, put them out in the sun, and dry them.
(Thomas R. "Blue" Fulford, Cortez, 1993, Jepson 1995)

Nets were designed so that the little bitty stuff could go through and we'd catch the ones that were big enough for our use.
(Thomas R. "Blue" Fulford, Cortez, 1993, Jepson 1995)

They were limed and spread after use to prevent rotting. Stop nets were tarred so the crabs couldn't eat them up.
(Bo Smith, Boca Grande, 1990, Edic 1996) (figure 14.7)

Most of them [stop nets] were made of cotton, and they took and put them in tar to preserve them. The crabs ate them anyway, but not quite as bad.
(Esperanza Woodring, Sanibel Island, 1990, Edic 1996)

They used stop nets to go along the edge, like on that island over there. When the tide is low, all of that goes dry in there underneath those mangroves. They would get in there with a dip net or a cast net [to remove the trapped fish].
(Esperanza Woodring, Sanibel Island, 1990, Edic 1996)

When my father first came down here [1890s] and started fishing, all the floats were wood. They were made out of something like gumbo limbo; they are real light. In later years when they started getting Spanish corks, he did not use them anymore.
(Tom Parkinson, Boca Grande, 1990, Edic 1996)

We make our paddles [net mesh gauges] out of wood. Sam Woodring made that one out of red mangrove root. I do not know why he used the red mangrove. I guess he used it because he thought it preserved or kept better.
(Esperanza Woodring, Sanibel Island, 1992, Edic 1996)

𝕺𝕺𝕺𝕺𝕺𝕺𝕺

Figure 14.7. Nets limed and hung to dry as Coleman and Padilla family members head out to visit relatives, Charlotte Harbor, 1920s. (Photo courtesy of Richard Coleman.)

Recent Indian Fishing in South Florida

Although most Indian people in Florida had been forced to move west in the 1840s, several hundred retreated into the Everglades and Big Cypress Swamp. Rivers and lakes provided them with foods such as fish, turtles, and alligators (figures 14.8 and 14.9). Today's south Florida Indian people recall seeing such activities by their parents and grandparents.

Mary Frances Johns recalled:

> They used fish poisons. . . . It made the fish drunk and come to the surface. . . . They tickled fish too. That was another way. You could stand in the water, in the clear water, and watch. You had your hands down there, and the fish comes along and you grab it from the bottom. . . . You just grab it and throw it out on the shore. (Consultants 1995)

Billy Cypress remembered, "My mother-in-law, she told somebody 'Watch out for the alligators, I'm going to dive for the turtles,' and she did. . . . The water turtles are the best eating" (Consultants 1995).

The Future of Coastal Fishing in Florida

The Calusa and their predecessors took plenty of fish from Florida's coastal waters. The Calusa thrived, becoming rich, powerful, and artistic. The Indian population was never so large that it seriously endangered the resources. But in the past fifty years the health of Florida's coastal waters has declined, and the estuaries are in trouble. Why? Here are four possible answers:

- Florida's exploding population is stretching coastal resources to their limits.
- We destroy fish habitat with polluting runoff from industry, farms, and fertilized lawns and by dredging and filling for development.
- Our boats pollute the water and damage sea grass meadows.
- We have replaced mangrove shorelines with concrete seawalls and lawns, eliminating habitat necessary for fish and other marine life.

Some people think that the decline in fish populations is due to over-fishing by commercial net fishers. But commercial fishers say that they are few in number and that they provide a valuable service by catching fresh fish for the public.

Other people believe that the vast increase in sport fishing, using advanced fishing equipment, has placed too much pressure on fish populations. Increasing habitat damage from too many boats may also be to blame. Certainly a small minority of fishing people—commercial and sport alike—have

Figure 14.8. A Seminole man with a freshly speared turtle. (Photo by Louis Capron, ca. 1930s; courtesy of Special Collections, University of Florida Libraries.)

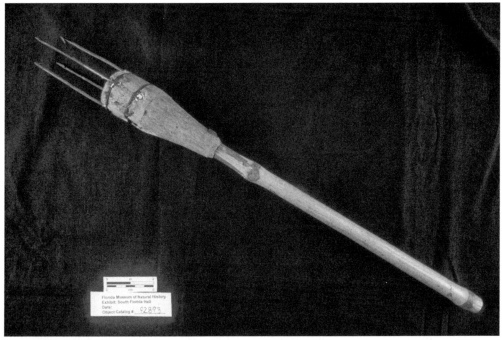

Figure 14.9. A Miccosukee Indian gig, 1950. The original handle was much longer. (Photo by Jeff Gage.)

Figure 14.10. A modern development in southwest Florida. (Photo by William Marquardt.)

selfishly abused fish resources. But most people who fish understand that the resources are finite and that some controls and limits are necessary.

Some think that the real issue is damage to the estuaries. They say that there would be plenty of fish for all if we could only control problems of pollution and habitat destruction. Estuaries are remarkably resilient and can absorb and filter heavy influxes of pollutants before suffering irreversible damage. Yet the estuaries are still declining. Why?

There is no doubt that we are capable of doing far more damage more quickly with modern machinery and pollutants from industry, agriculture, and lawn fertilizer than the Calusa could ever have dreamed of. For example, in the 1990s about twenty acres of Florida's forests, wetlands, and agricultural lands were converted to urban use every hour of every day.

The main driving factor in the deterioration of Florida's estuaries is the state's booming population. Nearly a thousand people move permanently to Florida each day, and only two hundred move away. Over 70 million people visit the state annually as tourists. More people means more boats, more fishing, more urban development, more pollution, and more waste (figure 14.10). Florida's natural resources cannot sustain such increases forever. Water quality, environmental diversity, and other environmental issues loom large in the state's future.

The Calusa and Their Legacy

❧❧❧❧❧❧

Gulf Coast Aquaculture

Some fisherfolk have turned to new ways to harvest the sea (figure 14.11). Aquaculture is the cultivation of animals and plants that live in water. But the success of aquaculture will also depend on good water quality and habitat preservation.

❧❧❧❧❧❧❧

Figure 14.11. Cedar Key clam farmer Chris Taiani and University of Florida aquaculture agent Leslie Sturmer shake silt from a clam bag, late 1990s. (Photo by Thomas Wright, University of Florida Institute of Food and Agricultural Sciences.)

Will there be fish in Florida's future? Or will we see the end of the 6,000-year fishing tradition in our own lifetimes? One thing for certain is that the fish and shellfish populations cannot survive destruction of their habitats. As mangroves, sea grasses, and other plants and animals are destroyed, so are the animals that depend on them for food and sanctuary. Only conscious human action can save Florida's estuaries for the future.

ⓑⓑⓑⓑⓑⓑ

15

Indian People in South Florida Today

Calusa society had all but faded from view by the mid 1700s, but other Indian people moved into their former south Florida domain. Today's south Florida Native Americans are culturally different from the Calusa and their neighbors and do not claim to be Calusa or to understand Calusa culture. But they have lived on their predecessors' lands during the last two centuries and are in that sense the inheritors of a "sense of place," a geography that defined early south Florida cultures (figure 15.1).

There are two federally recognized Indian tribes in south Florida today—the Seminole Tribe of Florida (about 3,000 members) and the Miccosukee Tribe of Indians of Florida (about 500 members) (figure 15.2)—as well as the unaffiliated Independent or Traditional Seminoles. The division between the tribes has more to do with the politics of federal recognition than with culture. The Seminoles and Miccosukees share a similar history and practice similar cultural traditions. Yet there are two distinct language groups among these peoples. Miccosukee people speak the Mikasuki (or Hitchiti) language. About two-thirds of Florida Seminole people speak the Mikasuki language, and the rest speak "Creek" (or Muskogee). These two languages are related but are not mutually intelligible. Some Miccosukee and Seminole people speak both languages, while others speak just one.

The Seminole and Miccosukee people have survived centuries of war, cultural upheaval, and oppression. In spite of the odds, they have a vibrant living culture that both retains traditional cultural values and charts new paths into the future.

Origins

Ancestors of the Seminole and Miccosukee people had lived in the lower Southeast for many thousands of years. When Europeans invaded America, southeastern Indian people suffered tremendous population loss and cultural disintegration from new diseases, warfare, and slavery. Determined to

Figure 15.1. The new generation—Frankie Billie, member of the Miccosukee Tribe of Indians of Florida, Miccosukee Reservation, 1998. (Photo by William Marquardt.)
Figure 15.2. Many Seminole and Miccosukee

people live on tribal reservations (locations shown on this map). (Graphic by Roger Mallot.)

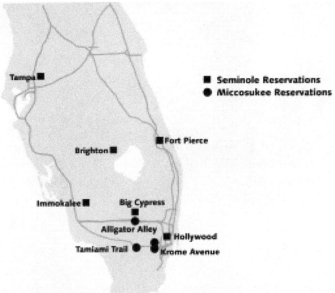

survive, many Indian people joined together. Some moved into the Florida peninsula, particularly people from present-day Georgia and Alabama whom the English collectively called "Creeks" (figure 15.3). They were joined by remnant populations of Florida native peoples and by Africans who had escaped from colonial slavery.

Spaniards referred to these people as *cimarrones*, meaning wild or untamed. Among the Indian people, this word became "Simanóli." Later, U.S. citizens called all Florida Indians "Seminole." Contemporary Seminole people reflect on the meaning of the word "Simanóli," as Billy Cypress noted, "As long as I remember, Simanóli was a word, in early Mikasuki, that de-

Figure 15.3. Engraving of an eighteenth-century Seminole leader in Florida, "Mico Chlucco the Long Warrior, or King of the Siminoles," published by William Bartram in 1793. (Courtesy of Special Collections, University of Florida Libraries.)

scribes wild things, or that which lives in the woods, of nature" (Consultants 1995). Mary Frances Johns added, "In other words, the idea is freedom. It's very precious to these people, and they do not wish to lose it" (Consultants 1995).

Wars and Removals

Between 1817 and 1858 the United States waged three aggressive campaigns against the Seminole people—the "Seminole Wars"—in an attempt to destroy their power and allow for colonization of territories coveted by whites. The United States government forcibly deported more than 3,000 Seminoles to Oklahoma, shipping them west by sea across the Gulf of Mexico from Tampa Bay (figure 15.4). This was part of a larger federal attempt to remove all Indian people in the eastern United States to "Indian Territory" west of the Mississippi River. Bolstered by the Indian Removal Act passed by Congress in 1830, the government forcibly deported nearly 100,000 Native Americans across brutal overland routes in what has become known as the "Trail of Tears" removal campaign. Today descendants of the Seminoles who went west are members of the Seminole Nation of Oklahoma.

∾∾∾∾∾∾

The Origin of People

They say the Maker of Breath was bored, so he came down and saw this place. It was going to be the earth, and it was like heated, molten rock. He took that and fixed it so that it would give a foundation for something to live on. Then he started building and fixing these gardens into this earth. The more he worked at it, the more beautiful the place became.

So he'd created this earth and it was so beautiful, but something had to be enjoying it. So he started creating animals. He started making them from clay and he would fix it so that these animals could breathe and walk around, and he had all these things created and he could not, for the life of him, figure out what was missing. But there was something missing. There were fishes in the water, birds in the air, animals on the land, so what in the whole creation was missing?

Then one day, he was sitting around the garden all by himself and then he realized, I am lonely. I need somebody to keep me company. That was what was missing. So he set about to make a person. He would make one person out of wood, and it didn't work, another out of something else, and it didn't work. Finally, he went back to using clay like he did with the animals and he made a person. He was baking it to cook it and he cooked it too long. It was too dark, so OK, he gave him breath and set him on his own territory.

Then he baked another one and it was under-baked, it was too white, and so he put that one in his own territory to live too, since this was a big world. So he baked another one and it was just right, so he put it in another area. The one that was just right, not too light or too dark, was the one that the Indians came from. All the Mexicans, Spanish, Chinese, and such came from different ones that were set in each area. So this is how we were created, they say. (Mary Frances Johns, Consultants 1995)

∾∾∾∾∾∾

The Unconquered

The Seminole and Miccosukee people who live in south Florida today are descendants of a few hundred people who evaded government capture and survived in the remote south Florida wilderness (figure 15.5). What does it mean to be Seminole?

Madelaine Tongkeamha explained, "I have my own language and I may have ways that are a little different. That is my right to live in that manner. It's my heritage, and I'll always have that" (Interviews 2000).

Figure 15.4.
*Sorrows of the
Seminoles—Ban-
ished from Florida.*
(Courtesy of Florida
State Archives.)

Samuel Tommie said, "To be a Seminole is to be proud to be a group of people that have made a great stand. Once you're born a Seminole, you're always a Seminole" (Interviews 2000).

Mary Frances Johns added, "I am a Seminole, like they say, by the grace of God, because I was born into it. And I am thankful every day for who I am. It is a way of being. It is a way of life" (Interviews 2000).

The Archaeology and History of the Seminoles in North Florida

Most people associate the Seminoles with the Everglades of south Florida. But during the eighteenth and early nineteenth centuries, the Seminoles lived in north Florida until forced farther south by aggressive military campaigns. Archaeologists have studied several Seminole villages dating to the 1700s and early 1800s. Artifacts from everyday life help describe community activities. During this period, Seminole communities changed from large traditional villages to small extended family camps based on clan affiliation.

"Town of the White King"

Before 1770 the Town of the White King on the Suwannee River was one of several major Seminole communities in Florida. The name "White King" probably derived from the Creek "white chiefs" who ruled over civil matters,

Figure 15.5b. Samuel Tommie. (Courtesy of Florida Museum of Natural History.)

Figure 15.5a. Madelaine Tongkeamha. (Courtesy of Florida Museum of Natural History.)

Figure 15.5c. Mary Frances Johns. (Courtesy of Florida Museum of Natural History.)

while "red chiefs" ruled over war. At the Town of the White King, archaeologists found traditional objects such as brushed pottery that reflect the residents' roots in Alabama and Georgia, while European goods illustrate the community's contact with colonial officials and traders (plate 47 and fig-ure 15.6).

English politician and plantation owner Denys Rolle described his visit to the town during a journey from east Florida to Pensacola in 1765:

I alighted at one of the first huts, but was soon after sent for by the head Man of that Tribe, who bears the Name of the White King. I went immediately to his Hut, and found him, with six or seven other stout Indians, sitting on their Couches of Repose. The Chief enquired of the Reason of our Journey, and at first seemed to object to our proceeding farther; but after some Time, he seemed to say nothing further. Soon after there was served up some Venison dressed with Bear's Oil, and a Bowl of China-Briar-Root soup. They invited me up to a Dance, which they use on the Arrival of Strangers, and the whole Village joined in it till about Eleven o'Clock. The Chiefs came down likewise, and they seemed to be also in a very agreeable Humour. (Rolle 1977)

Trading Posts

Prior to the Seminole Wars and especially during the late 1700s, Seminole people actively engaged in trade with Europeans, and trading posts became focal points for material and cultural exchange. Seminoles traded animal skins and farm produce such as rice, corn, pumpkins, peaches, and melons for European goods such as fabric, horse tack, knives, jewelry, guns, and ammunition. Objects from Spalding's Lower Store, established in the 1770s on the St. Johns River near Palatka, reflect some of the goods available to the Seminoles (figure 15.7).

Figure 15.6. Archaeologist John Goggin recovers a Seminole brushed pot during work at Oven Hill (the vessel is pictured in plate 47).

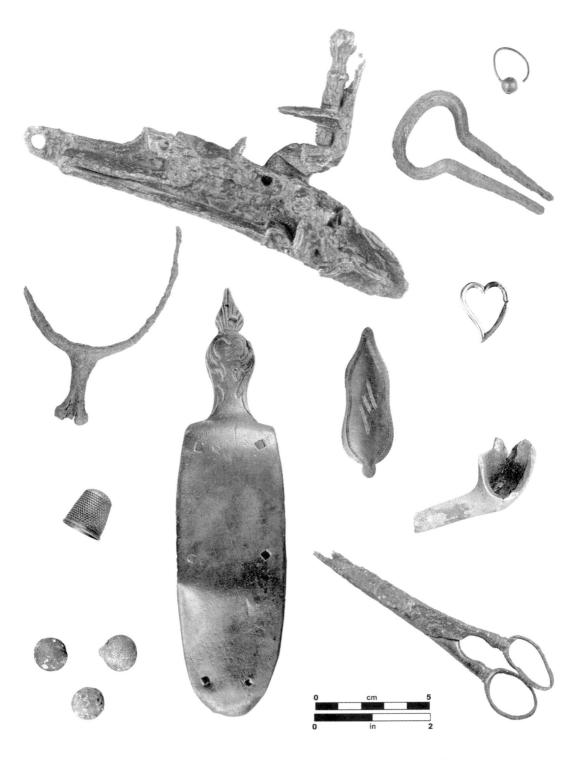

Figure 15.7. Objects from Spalding's Lower Store site, clockwise from upper left: musket flintlock, mouth harp, earring, heart-shaped brooch, trigger guard, clay pipe fragment, scissors, musket butt plate, lead shot, thimble, spur frame. (Photos by Jeff Gage, graphic by Pat Payne.)

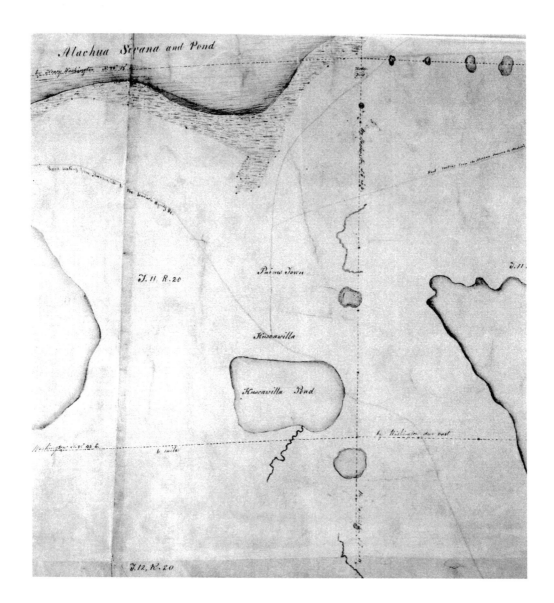

Figure 15.8. Map of the Arredondo Grant showing "Paines Town" and "Kuscawilla," Henry Washington, 1833. (Courtesy of National Archives and Records Administration, College Park, MD, RG 49, Old Map File, Florida 2a, 2b.)

Cuscowilla and King Payne's Town

In the late 1700s the major Seminole community in the Gainesville area was Cuscowilla, located on the edge of Paynes Prairie near today's Micanopy (figure 15.8). The exact location of Cuscowilla remains unknown.

The town of Cuscowilla, which is the capital of the Alachua tribe, contains about thirty habitations, each of which consists of two houses nearly the same size, about thirty feet in length, twelve feet wide, and about the same in height. . . . A pretty brook of water ran through the town, and entered the lake just by. We were welcomed to the town, and conducted by the young men and maidens to the chief's house, which stood on an eminence, and was distinguished from the rest by its superior magnitude. The chief, who is called the Cowkeeper, attended by several ancient men, came to us. We followed him to an apartment prepared for the reception of their guests. The repast consisted of venison, stewed with bear's oil, fresh corn cakes, milk, and homony; and our drink, honey and water, very cool and agreeable. (Bartram 1791; 1955)

When leader Cowkeeper died in the 1790s, a younger relative referred to as "King Payne" assumed leadership and moved the town north along the prairie rim (figure 15.9). In 1812 King Payne was wounded in a skirmish with a Georgia militia assigned to destroy Indian towns near Alachua. He later died, and the town was abandoned; but the name remains with us today—Paynes Prairie.

Clan Camps and War Camps

During the Seminole Wars, large Seminole towns gave way to small, dispersed clan camps composed of related women from the same clan and their families (figure 15.10). Separate camps developed as men involved in the wars moved strategically from place to place. In the Second Seminole War,

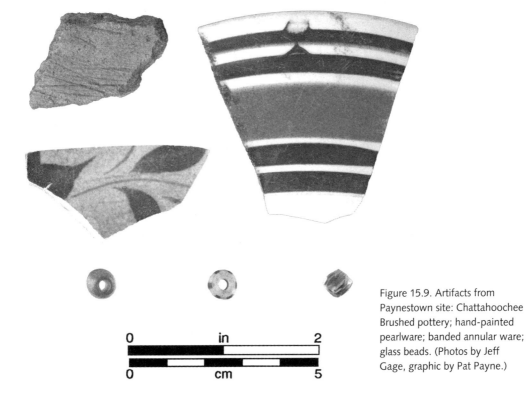

Figure 15.9. Artifacts from Paynestown site: Chattahoochee Brushed pottery; hand-painted pearlware; banded annular ware; glass beads. (Photos by Jeff Gage, graphic by Pat Payne.)

Figure 15.10. Objects from two clan camps in Citrus County, 1830s: (top) two brushed pottery sherds; (lower left) lead shot; (lower right) U.S. military button. (Photos by Jeff Gage, graphic by Pat Payne.)

the famous Seminole leader Osceola (sometimes called Powell) and his followers established a village in the Withlacoochee swamps of Citrus County near today's town of Inverness (figure 15.11). Very few remnants mark the spot of "Powell's Town," occupied for a short time during 1835 and 1836 until the villagers fled to avoid pursuit by the American military.

The "Black Seminoles": African Allies

The people who came to be known as "Black Seminoles" were Africans who escaped from slavery in the English colonies, fled to Spanish Florida, and allied themselves with Seminole Indian people (figure 15.12). These African allies of the Seminole people created a culture of their own and reshaped relations among people of Indian, black, and European descent.

The Black Seminoles established towns near and sometimes with their Indian allies and often served as interpreters and negotiators between the Seminoles and Europeans. In the 1830s a Black Seminole named Abraham was among the most prominent of these leaders (figure 15.13). According to John Lee Williams in 1837, "Abraham has as much influence in the nation as

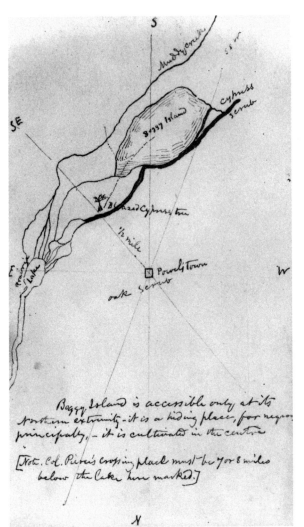

Figure 15.11. Sketch map showing location of Powell's Town, 1837, Henry Prince Diary. (Courtesy of Special Collections, University of Florida Libraries.)

Figure 15.12. Historic map showing locations of Black Seminole or "Negro Towns" on the Suwannee River, destroyed by Andrew Jackson in 1818. (Courtesy of National Archives and Records Administration, College Park, MD, RG 77, L247-94.)

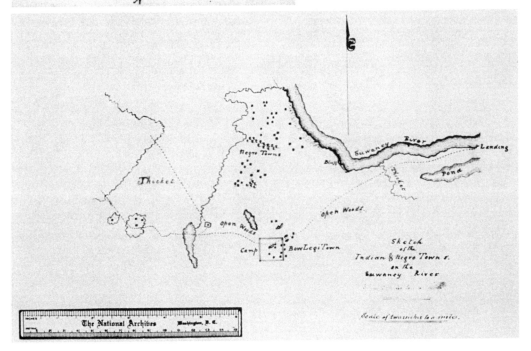

"BILLY BOWLEGS," AND HIS SUITE OF INDIAN CHIEFS.—FROM A DAGUERREOTYPE BY MEADE, BROTHERS, NEW YORK.—(SEE PRECEDING PAGE.)

Figure 15.13. Engraving titled "Billy Bowlegs and His Suite of Indian Chiefs" in New York, 1853, printed in the *Illustrated London News*. Abraham is in back row, center. (Courtesy of Special Collections, University of Florida Libraries.)

BEN BRUNO, NEGRO SLAVE AND FAVORITE.

Figure 15.14. Ben Bruno, confidant of Chief Billy Bowlegs, was interpreter and advisor to the Seminoles, as depicted in *Harper's Weekly*, 1858. (Courtesy of Special Collections, University of Florida Libraries.)

Figure 15.15. The Reverend B. A. Newton is a great-grandson of Black Seminole Moses Newton, who left Florida for the Bahamas in 1821. Today about 250 Black Seminole descendants still live in the small settlement of Red Bays on Andros Island. (Photo by Rosalyn Howard.)

any other man. With an appearance of great modesty, he is ambitious, avaricious, and withal very intelligent" (Williams 1962).

Mayer Cohen wrote, "Under an exterior of profound meekness, Abraham . . . has at once the crouch and the spring of the panther" (Cohen 1836).

Nominally regarded as "slaves" to the Seminoles, the Africans provided their allies with a "tax" of agricultural produce but otherwise lived much as equals and political partners. The Seminoles valued their abilities as interpreters and relied on them as advisors and strategists as well as fighters and farmers (figure 15.14).

The relationship between Africans and Seminoles angered and frightened English colonists and later Americans. Many urged the government to use force to break up the African/Indian partnership, enslave the Black Seminoles, and remove the Indians west of the Mississippi. The United States tried to coerce the Seminoles to move west but reached no agreement. Hostilities erupted at the end of 1835, and the Second Seminole War raged for seven years—the longest, most costly, and deadliest war ever fought between the United States and Native Americans. Through both forced truce and capture,

Figure 15.16. *The Burning of Peliklikaha.* (Painting by General Abraham Eustis, 1836; courtesy of Library of Congress.)

the U.S. government deported most Black Seminoles along with other Seminole people to the Indian Territories in Oklahoma.

Today descendants of these African allies still live in Oklahoma, Texas, and Mexico. Some Black Seminoles migrated from Florida to the Caribbean, and their descendants continue to live on Andros Island in the Bahamas (figure 15.15). Reverend B. A. Newton related, "In ones and twos, in their dugout canoes, the Negro Seminoles crossed the Gulf Stream and landed along the western shore of Andros from the Joulter Cays south over a twenty year period. They congregated at Red Bays" (Howard 2002).

ⓖⓖⓖⓖⓖⓖⓖ

On the Trail of the Black Seminoles

Little is known about Black Seminoles in Florida because their survival depended on their ability to elude capture or notice, and they left few written records. Recent research has employed the tools of history, oral history, and archaeology to reconstruct the Black Seminole story.

Researchers have identified the location of Peliklikaha—a prominent Black Seminole town during the early 1800s, located in today's Sumter County (figure 15.16). Peliklikaha was home to Abraham, the renowned Black Seminole interpreter. Seminole chief Micanopy, with whom Abraham collaborated throughout the Seminole Wars, probably resided there at least part-time. Archaeologists have excavated fragments from everyday life, which indicate that the residents lived much as their Seminole allies and neighbors did (figure 15.17).

ⓖⓖⓖⓖⓖⓖⓖ

Figure 15.17. Artifacts from Peliklikaha. (Photo by Pat Payne.)

16

ᕲᕲᕲᕲᕲᕲ

Seminole and Miccosukee Culture and Arts

Seminole and Miccosukee people prevailed over years of oppression and challenges to their survival and are alive and well in south Florida today—a thoroughly modern people steeped in traditional cultural practices. Both tribes actively engage in a wide range of economic enterprises. Perhaps best known for their lucrative gambling casinos, they also operate cattle ranches, citrus groves, construction companies, an Everglades Restoration Initiative, a broadcasting service, a tribal newspaper, schools and health services, tourist attractions, and educational enterprises such as the Ah Tah Thi Ki Museum and the Miccosukee Indian Museum (figures 16.1–16.4).

While fully involved in contemporary society, Seminole and Miccosukee people still hold older traditions at the heart of their culture. Let's take a brief look at some of these traditions.

Figure 16.1. Rudy Osceola rounds up cattle, 1998. (Photo by Michael James, courtesy of Seminole Communications, Seminole Tribe of Florida.)

Figure 16.2. Seminole headquarters. (Photo by Darcie MacMahon.)

Figure 16.3. Miccosukee headquarters. (Photo by David Harlos.)

Figure 16.4. Max Osceola Jr. and Mitchell Cypress congratulate Jessica Turtle upon her Head Start graduation, 1996. (Courtesy of Seminole Communications, Seminole Tribe of Florida.)

Clothing

The Seminoles and Miccosukees are perhaps best known for their colorful clothing. In the 1800s and early 1900s women decorated clothing with appliquéd designs, applied after the garment was made. By 1880 hand-operated sewing machines had appeared in Seminole camps, and clothing designs became more complex. In the early 1900s seamstresses added colorful horizontal stripes to clothing (plate 48). By the 1920s they had developed their famous patchwork designs, which were sewn directly into the garment instead of being applied.

Patchwork designs range from simple to complex, but all rely on the same basic technique. The artist sews strips of cloth together, cuts the combined strips into sections, repositions them, and sews them together in the new position (plate 49).

Clothing and patchwork designs have evolved over the years. Men's garments changed from simple full-cut shirts and "long shirt" coats to "big shirts" with a fitted waistband and finally to jackets and sport shirts with bands of patchwork. Women's clothing also changed, featuring different styles of skirt decoration and capes of various lengths.

The patchwork tradition is very much alive today. Many Seminole and Miccosukee men and women wear patchwork clothing, sometimes daily and sometimes only for special occasions. Patchwork artists exhibit and sell their work at tribal fairs and other community events (plate 50).

Dolls

Seminole and Miccosukee women made dolls for the tourist trade throughout the twentieth century and still make them today (plate 51). Materials and techniques have varied, but most dolls are made of sewn and stuffed saw-palmetto trunk fiber and are adorned with patchwork clothing. Doll makers are traditionally women past menopause. There are fewer people making dolls today, and it is increasingly difficult to harvest palmetto. In spite of this, the tradition persists—and dolls remain popular with both tourists and collectors.

Basketry

Basketry has been an important art among southeastern Indian people for thousands of years. Early Seminole and Miccosukee baskets were made of split cane or palmetto stems woven into herringbone, diamond, or other designs. The most common forms include sifting baskets and trays for processing corn and pack baskets for carrying food or other goods. Coiled sweet-grass baskets became common during the first half of the twentieth century. Today they are the dominant form and often include decorative elements such as palmetto doll heads and colorful stitching (plate 52). Basketry is mostly a woman's art. Seminole basketmaker Mary Frances Johns reflected on the art of basket making:

> In a way my baskets are like my children. They are something that you work on for so long. Making baskets is like painting a picture. It's a time of relaxation where I can just sit and keep my hands busy and my thoughts elsewhere. It's a time of thinking and it's a time of introspection into my own self and my own being. So I guess you could say it can be a spiritual experience. (Interviews 2000) (plate 53)

Woodwork

Woodworking, typically a man's art, traditionally encompassed construction of the family chickee (house) and the all-important dugout canoe, the making of ball-game racquets and men's dance rattles, and the whittling of animal figurines and model canoes for the tourist trade. Woodworkers also made everyday household items such as corn mortars and pestles, coontie root graters (for the tuber of the coontie plant, *Zamia integrifolia*), fish and turtle gigs, and large spoons for sofkee (a traditional corn soup). Although fewer men practice woodworking today, the tradition is still alive (figure 16.5).

Figure 16.5. Henry John Billie, traditional canoe carver, works on a cypress canoe, 1996. (Photo by Darcie Mac-Mahon.)

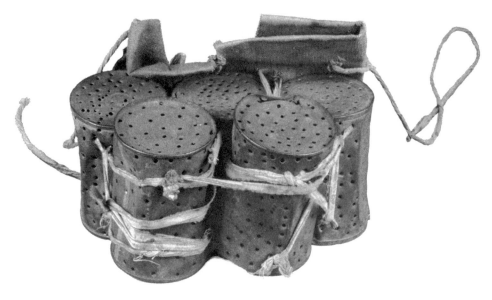

Figure 16.6. Women's dance rattles: (top) metal cans (ca. 1930); (bottom) box turtle (1926–27). (Photos by Jeff Gage, graphic by Pat Payne.)

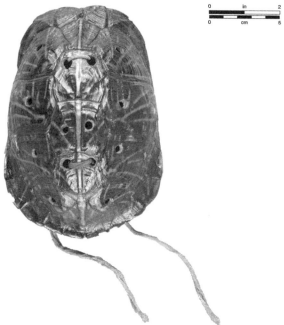

Women's Dance Rattles

Seminole and Miccosukee women wear rattles on their legs during traditional dances. Rattles made of metal cans replaced the traditional turtle-shell rattles in the twentieth century (figure 16.6). Dancers filled both rattles with the seeds of the native canna lily. Mary Frances Johns commented, "People always think of us wearing these turtle shell rattles. But the cans are more comfortable to wear, and they make a nicer sound. You can always tell where someone has emptied her rattles. You'll see a stand of canna lilies growing in that spot" (Consultants 1995).

Silverwork

Seminole silverworking was traditionally a man's art practiced most actively during the nineteenth and early twentieth centuries. Silversmiths fashioned European coins into ornaments for both men and women and were influenced by both European trade items and precolumbian copperwork from the Southeast. The simplest technique was to pierce coins for use in necklaces or earrings. More complex bossed ornaments were made by heating a coin, hammering it flat on an axe-head anvil, cutting the shape, and using antlers or other sharp objects to emboss a design. Sometimes the design was carved

Figure 16.7. Alice Willie Osceola and her daughter Mittie, around 1917–19. Alice wears silver brooches on her cape and a single pierced pendant from her hair. (Photo by Frank A. Robinson; courtesy of Smithsonian Institution, National Anthropological Archives.)

on a wooden stump, and the silversmith hammered the metal on the stump to create the embossed relief. Pierced ornaments were made by cutting designs into a flattened coin, sometimes using a chisel (figures 16.7 and 16.8). Mary Frances Johns observed:

> The women wore their wealth. They rarely left it off. . . . Men did this kind of work for their women. You rarely ever saw a woman make these things. There were men who were particularly skillful and talented at it, so some would commission other men to make them for them. Women would ask them to make things for them. Fathers and uncles would make silver for little girls, so girls would have the beginnings of a collection. Some women had two sets of silver and beads. One you acquired as a child and the other you acquired as a married woman as your husband bought you things. (Consultants 1995)

Today silverworking is virtually a lost art, although several individuals are attempting to revive the tradition, often with a modern flair.

Beadwork

Beads have figured prominently in Seminole and Miccosukee decorative arts and have always been important to southeastern peoples. Throughout Native America, European glass trade beads largely replaced precolumbian beads made of shell, bone, and other natural materials. Prior to the nineteenth-century Seminole Wars, both Seminole men and women wore strung glass beads. Women also worked glass beads into men's clothing, including nineteenth-century fabric leggings and shoulder bags (plate 54) and beaded belts or shoulder sashes. Well into the twentieth century, Seminole women commonly wore enormous numbers of beaded necklaces. Today women create new forms of beaded bracelets and necklaces, and a very few individuals have given new life to the art of beaded shoulder bags.

Fingerweaving

Fingerweaving is a technique of interlacing yarns onto a small hand-held loom by using fingers rather than a shuttle. This art form was common among all southeastern peoples in the eighteenth and nineteenth centuries.

Figure 16.9. Old Tallahassee wearing fingerwoven sash and garters and beaded shoulder bag, about 1900. (Courtesy of Historical Museum of Southern Florida.)

Figure 16.10. Jay McGirt (Oklahoma Seminole) fingerweaving, 2002. (Photo by Darcie MacMahon.)

Seminole and Miccosukee women produced fingerwoven sashes, garters, belts, and other specialized clothing for men. They sometimes embellished the decorative woven designs with beads (figure 16.9 and plate 55). Finger-weaving is largely a vanished tradition; however, inspired by a renewed interest in traditional arts, a very small number of people have begun relearning and practicing this venerable art (figure 16.10).

Kinship and Clans

Among Seminoles and Miccosukees, kinship passes through the women. Children are born into their mother's *clan* or extended family group. A man marries into his wife's clan and traditionally went to live in the wife's clan camp. Today there are eight clans: Bear, Snake, Panther, Bigtown, Bird, Deer, Wind, and Otter (figure 16.11). Other clans, such as Alligator, are now extinct in Florida because the last female member died. Some additional clans live on among the people of the Seminole Nation of Oklahoma.

Housing

Traditional Seminole and Miccosukee houses, called chickees, are constructed of cypress log frames covered with palm thatch roofs. Today most people live in modern homes but still enjoy traditional chickees for family

Figure 16.11. The eight contemporary clans of the Seminoles. (Drawing by Merald Clark.)

gatherings or special-purpose buildings. Specialized builders preserve the time-honored craft of chickee construction, and their creations range from small playground structures to fantastic community buildings (figure 16.12).

Food

Today most traditional cooking occurs on special occasions, although fry bread and sofkee are still common (figure 16.13). Sofkee is a hot drink or soup made of corn grits or roasted corn. In the past, a pot of sofkee or other hot soup would simmer all day on the fire for people to help themselves when they were hungry. Swamp cabbage (the heart of the cabbage palm), bread made from coontie flour (from the Zamia plant's root), turtle, garfish, and other wild foods also graced the Seminole and Miccosukee menu.

Figure 16.12. Large chickee at Billie Swamp Safari, Big Cypress Reservation, Seminole Tribe of Florida, 1997. (Photo by Darcie MacMahon.)

Figure 16.13. Jenny Shore makes Seminole fry bread. (Courtesy of Seminole Communications, Seminole Tribe of Florida.)

Figure 16.14. Medicine man Bobby Henry leads a Seminole dance. (Courtesy of Seminole Communications, Seminole Tribe of Florida.)

Language

There are two distinct languages among the Seminole: Mikasuki (sometimes called Hitchiti) and Creek (also called Muskogee). Miccosukee people speak Mikasuki. About two-thirds of the Seminole speak Mikasuki, and one-third speak Creek. Some people are fluent in both languages, and most people also speak English. The Seminoles and Miccosukees are committed to preserving and teaching the traditional languages to their children. Mary Frances Johns said, "Your language is the most important part of your culture because it is an identifier for your people. It identifies you as a tribe, as a people, as a culture unto yourself. So once you lose that, then you're open to losing everything else" (Interviews 2000).

Oral Traditions

Until recent years, Seminole and Miccosukee history has been strictly an oral tradition. Oral traditions recount historical events, convey values, or explain the nature of the world. Oral history is still a valuable way for elders to pass information to children and other tribal members (plate 56).

Ceremonies

The Seminoles and Miccosukees still practice traditional ceremonies, the most important of which is the annual Green Corn Dance. This is a private tribal event where dances, purification and manhood ceremonies, traditional medicine ceremonies, and resolution of disputes take place. Although non-Indians cannot attend Green Corn, the public can enjoy public Seminole dance performances at events such as folk festivals and powwows (figure 16.14).

Medicine

Traditional healers still play a vital role in Seminole and Miccosukee society (figure 16.15). These medicine men and women do not replace Western medical doctors but instead complement Western medicine. They use natural ingredients and other customs to treat a wide variety of physical and mental disorders. Traditional medicine can also influence a person's decisions, success, safety, and other life issues. Tribal members usually do not discuss most details about traditional medicine outside the tribe.

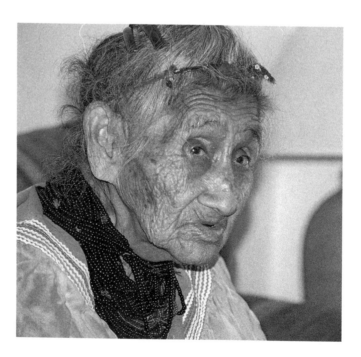

Figure 16.15. Medicine woman Susie Billie. (Courtesy of Seminole Communications, Seminole Tribe of Florida.)

ⓖⓖⓖⓖⓖⓖ

17

The Future of South Florida

South Florida's human history is a richly woven tapestry of varied traditions: the Calusa and their neighbors, Spanish and English colonists, Spanish fisherfolk who came from Cuba in the 1700s, Seminole and Miccosukee people who arrived later and continue to flourish, and today's many diverse residents who enjoy life in the area. All of these cultures and their histories have contributed to the Florida that we know, and the telling of their stories gives context to our lives and a framework for making decisions.

It is commonly said that ancient Indian people were close to their environment and that contemporary people are not. But such a romantic vision of Indian people belies their humanity. As human beings, ancient Indian people acted on the knowledge that they had available to them and modified their environment in ways that made sense to them, just as we do today.

The Calusa are the main characters in this book. The Calusa built houses to live in, made boats in which to travel, dug canals, mounded up dirt and shells to make earthworks, and produced prodigious amounts of garbage. Today we do the same things. Was it right when the Calusa did these things but wrong when we do them today? Of course not. But the ancient Calusa manipulated their surroundings and exploited their environment and had no lasting ill effect on it. Why, then, are our estuaries and other parts of our environment in trouble today? What is different?

First, there are more of us than there were of them. More than 800 people move permanently to Florida each day (one person every 1.8 minutes), and tens of millions visit as tourists. From 1990 to 2000 Florida's population increased by 23.5 percent. For example, Cape Coral, a city in the former Calusa domain, increased from 34,167 in 1980 to 74,991 in 1990 to 102,286 in 2000. By 2025 Cape Coral's population is expected to be 245,637—a 140 percent increase in twenty-five years. Continued population increase, resource depletion, and habitat destruction threaten Florida's environments. Only purposeful human action will ensure that Florida continues to grow in ways that do not destroy the very resources that make it such an attractive place to live.

Figure 17.1. South Florida estuaries have supported people for thousands of years. (Photo by Jeff Ripple.)

Florida's resources are not infinite. Each day, the average Florida resident or visitor uses 175 gallons of water, compared with averages of 110 gallons in the United States, 52 in Great Britain, 39 in France, and 35 in Israel. Urbanization intensifies the water problem, because demand for water per acre increases as wetlands and citrus groves are turned into subdivisions and mobile-home communities. About half of Florida's water use is for agriculture, but lawn care accounts for millions of gallons per day and discharges pesticides and fertilizers into rivers, streams, and aquifers throughout the state. The constantly moving and changing estuaries filter this pollution in myriad ways, just as they have since the time of the Calusa. But they may not be able to keep pace if our population continues to increase and our practices do not change.

The second difference between the Calusa impact on the environment and ours is that our technology makes it seem as though we are less dependent on the environment because we experience it less intimately. With little daily contact and engagement with our natural surroundings, we have insufficient knowledge of the long-term implications of our activities, and thus it is easier to make serious mistakes. In this book we have shown how estuaries work and suggested that we all need to comprehend how our environment works for us, wherever we live. Once we do, environmental conservation makes good sense—it is good for our health, our safety, and our economy.

In this book we have focused mainly on the Calusa, a prosperous, influential, and artistic society. What was the secret of Calusa success? An intricate system of sea grasses and mangroves and a magical mixing of fresh and salt water—the estuary—provided food in such quantities that farming was never needed. Today these estuaries still offer us food, recreation, and beauty, but they need our help. The Calusa legacy lives on, inspiring us to learn about and care for the coastal environment that they called home.

Places to Visit

Florida Museum of Natural History
Near corner of Hull Road and SW 34th Street
On campus of the University of Florida
Gainesville, FL 32611
(352) 846-2000
www.flmnh.ufl.edu

Ah-Tah-Thi-Ki Museum
Seminole Tribe of Florida
Big Cypress Seminole Reservation
HC-61, Box 21-A
Clewiston, FL 33440
(863) 902-1113
www.seminoletribe.com/museum

Bailey-Matthews Shell Museum
3075 Sanibel-Captiva Road
Sanibel Island, FL 33957
(239) 395-2233
www.shellmuseum.org

Biscayne National Park
P.O. Box 1369
Homestead, FL 33090-1369
(305) 230-7275
www.biscayne.national-park.com

Collier County Museum
Collier County Government Complex
U.S. 41 and Airport-Pulling Road
Naples, FL 34102
(239) 774-8476
www.colliermuseum.com/museums

Everglades National Park
Various visitor locations in south Florida
Call the Shark Valley Visitor Center:
(305) 221-8776
www.nps.gov/ever

Florida Aquarium
701 Channelside Drive
Tampa, FL 33602
(813) 273-4000
www.flaquarium.org

Gulf Specimen Marine Laboratory
300 Clark Drive, P.O. Box 237
Panacea, FL 32346
(850) 984-5297
www.gulfspecimen.org

Historic Spanish Point
337 N. Tamiami Trail
Osprey, FL 34229
(941) 966-5214
www.historicspanishpoint.org

Historical Museum of Southern Florida
101 West Flagler Street
Miami, FL 33130
(305) 375-1492
www.historical-museum.org

Miccosukee Indian Village
P.O. Box 440021
Mile Marker 70
US 41—Tamiami Trail
Miami, FL 33144
(305) 223-8380
www.miccosukee.com/tribe.html

Mote Marine Laboratory
1600 Ken Thompson Parkway
Sarasota, FL 34236
(941) 388-4441
www.mote.org

Randell Research Center at Pineland
13810 Waterfront Drive, across from Tarpon Lodge
P.O. Box 608
Pineland, FL 33945
(239) 283-2062
e-mail: randellcenter@comcast.net
www.flmnh.ufl.edu/rrc

Seminole Okalee Indian Village and Museum
Seminole Tribe of Florida
Hard Rock Hotel and Casino
5731 S. State Road 7
Fort Lauderdale, FL 33314
(954) 965-2424
www.seminoletribe.com/enterprises/hollywood/okalee.
shtml

South Florida Museum
201 10th Street West
Bradenton, FL 34205
(941) 746-4131
www.southfloridamuseum.org/

Trail of the Lost Tribes
Write for free brochure:
Trail of the Lost Tribes Project
1815 Palma Sola Blvd.
Bradenton, FL 34209
(941) 794-8773

Suggested Readings

Resources for Teachers

Lesson plans on Florida archaeology and history

Write to:
Florida Heritage Education Program
Division of Historical Resources
500 South Bronough Street
Tallahassee, FL 32399-0250

Guide to the Pineland Site for teachers

Payne, Claudine, and Charles Blanchard. *Archaeology and Environment at the Pineland Site Complex: Information and Activities for 4th and 5th Grade Teachers.* Gainesville: University of Florida Institute of Archaeology and Paleoenvironmental Studies, 1997.
Write to: IAPS Books, P.O. Box 117800, Gainesville, FL 32611.

Ecoventures: Learning in Florida's Environment

A multimedia program including hands-on and simulated labs, student reader, and educator's guide. Florida Department of Environmental Protection and Florida State University, 1995.
Contact: Interactive Media Science Project, Florida State University, Tallahassee, FL 32306-4490.

Inquiry Boxes: Museum on the Move

Inquiry boxes for loan or docent-guided use in north-central Florida counties, covering three subject matters: Seminole People, Northern Florida's Early Native People, Southern Florida's Early Native People. Includes teacher's guide and cultural objects.
See web site information at www.flmnh.ufl.edu or contact the Florida Museum of Natural History at tours@flmnh.ufl.edu, (352) 846-2000, ext. 214.

Florida's Environment

Carr, Archie. *A Naturalist in Florida: A Celebration of Eden.* Ed. by Marjorie Harris Carr. New Haven, Conn.: Yale University Press, 1994.

Florida's Fabulous (various). A series that includes books about *Birds, Butterflies, Insects, Mammals, Seashores,* etc. Tampa, Fla.: World Publications.

Myers, Ronald L., and John J. Ewel (eds.). *Ecosystems of Florida.* Gainesville: University Presses of Florida, 1990.

Rabkin, Richard, and Jacob Rabkin. *Nature Guide to Florida.* Miami, Fla.: Banyan Books, 1978.

The Archaeology and History of Southwest Florida

Blanchard, Charles E. *New Words, Old Songs: Understanding the Lives of Ancient Peoples in Southwest Florida through Archaeology.* Illustrated by Merald Clark. Gainesville: University of Florida Institute of Archaeology and Paleoenvironmental Studies, 1995.

Edic, Robert F. *Fisherfolk of Charlotte Harbor, Florida.* Gainesville: University of Florida Institute of Archaeology and Paleoenvironmental Studies, 1996.

Florida Museum of Natural History. *The Domain of the Calusa* (VHS video, 29 minutes). Gainesville: University of Florida Institute of Archaeology and Paleoenvironmental Studies, 1995.

The Archaeology and History of Florida

Brown, Robin C. *Florida's First People.* Sarasota, Fla.: Pineapple Press, 1994.

Gannon, Michael (ed.). *The New History of Florida.* Gainesville: University Press of Florida, 1996.

Hann, John H., and Bonnie G. McEwan. *The Apalachee Indians and Mission San Luis.* Gainesville: University Press of Florida, 1998.

Milanich, Jerald T. *Florida's Indians and the Invasion from Europe.* Gainesville: University Press of Florida, 1995.

———. *Florida's Indians from Ancient Times to the Present.* Gainesville: University Press of Florida, 1998.

———. *The Timucua.* Oxford: Blackwell, 1996.

Purdy, Barbara A. *Indian Art of Ancient Florida.* Gainesville: University Press of Florida, 1996.

Weisman, Brent R. *Unconquered People: Florida's Seminole and Miccosukee Indians.* Gainesville: University Press of Florida, 1999.

Florida Indian People Today

Downs, Dorothy. *Art of the Florida Seminole and Miccosukee Indians.* Gainesville: University Press of Florida, 1995.

Jumper, Betty Mae. *Legends of the Seminoles.* Illustrated by Guy LaBree. Sarasota, Fla.: Pineapple Press, 1994.

West, Patsy. *The Enduring Seminoles: From Alligator Wrestling to Ecotourism.* Gainesville: University Press of Florida, 1998.

Bibliography

Adair, James. *The History of the American Indians.* London, 1775.

Alevizon, William S. *Beachcomber's Guide to Florida Marine Life.* Houston, Tex.: Gulf Publishing Company, 1994.

Arnade, Charles W. "Raids, Sieges, and International Wars." In *The New History of Florida*, edited by Michael Gannon, 100–116. Gainesville: University Press of Florida, 1996.

Barrientos, Bartolomé. *Pedro Menéndez de Avilés, Founder of Florida.* Trans. Anthony Kerrigan. Gainesville: University of Florida Press, 1965.

Bartram, William. *Travels of William Bartram.* 1791. Reprint. Edited by Mark Van Doren. New York: Dover Publications, 1955.

Blackard, David M. *Patchwork and Palmettos: Seminole-Miccosukee Folk Art since 1820.* Fort Lauderdale, Fla.: Fort Lauderdale Historical Society, 1990.

Clark, Merald R. "Faces and Figureheads: The Masks of Prehistoric South Florida." Master's thesis, University of Florida, 1995.

Cohen, Mayer. *Notices of Florida and the Campaigns.* Charleston: Burges and Honour, 1836.

Coker, William S., and Susan R. Parker. "The Second Spanish Period in the Two Floridas." In *The New History of Florida*, edited by Michael Gannon, 150–66. Gainesville: University Press of Florida, 1996.

Consultants for exhibit planning, Hall of South Florida People and Environments. Unpublished typescript on file, Florida Museum of Natural History, University of Florida, Gainesville, 1995.

Covington, James W. "Trade Relations between Southwestern Florida and Cuba—1600–1840." *Florida Historical Quarterly* 38 (1959): 114–28.

Cushing, Frank Hamilton. "Exploration of Ancient Key Dweller Remains on the Gulf Coast of Florida." *American Philosophical Society, Proceedings* 35 (1897): 329–448. Reprinted, Gainesville: University Press of Florida, 2001.

Densmore, Frances. *Seminole Music.* Smithsonian Institution, Bureau of American Ethnology, Bulletin 161. Washington, D.C.: U.S. Government Printing Office, 1956.

Dickinson, Jonathan. *Jonathan Dickinson's Journal, or God's Protecting Providence, Being* the Narrative of a Journey from Port Royal in Jamaica to Philadelphia, August 23, 1696 to April 1st, 1697. Port Salerno: Florida Classics Library, 1985.

Downs, Dorothy. *Art of the Florida Seminole and Miccosukee Indians*. Gainesville: University Press of Florida, 1995.

Edic, Robert F. *Fisherfolk of Charlotte Harbor, Florida*. Gainesville: University of Florida, Institute of Archaeology and Paleoenvironmental Studies, 1996.

Ernst, Carl H., Jeffrey E. Lovich, and Roger W. Barbour. *Turtles of the United States and Canada*. Washington, D.C.: Smithsonian Institution Press, 1994.

Fontaneda, Do. d'Escalante. *Memoir of Do. d'Escalante Fontaneda Respecting Florida, Written in Spain, about the Year 1575*. Translated by Buckingham Smith and with editorial comments by D. O. True. Coral Gables, Fla.: Glades House, 1944.

Fotheringham, Nick, and Susan Brunenmeister. *Beachcomber's Guide to Gulf Coast Marine Life*. Houston, Tex.: Gulf Publishing, 1989.

Gilliland, Marion S. *Key Marco's Buried Treasure: Archaeology and Adventure in the Nineteenth Century*. Gainesville: University Presses of Florida, 1989.

———. *The Material Culture of Key Marco, Florida*. Gainesville: University Presses of Florida, 1975.

Goggin, John M., and William T. Sturtevant. "Calusa: A Stratified Non-Agricultural Society (with Notes on Sibling Marriage)." In *Explorations in Cultural Anthropology: Essays in Honor of George Peter Murdock*, edited by Ward Goodenough, 179–219. New York: McGraw-Hill, 1964.

Greenberg, Jerry, Idaz Greenberg, and Michael Greenberg. *Mangroves: Trees in the Sea*. Miami, Fla.: Seahawk Press, 2000.

Griffin, John. *The Archaeology of Everglades National Park: A Synthesis*. Tallahassee, Fla.: National Park Service, Southeastern Archeological Center, 1988. Annotated and reprinted, Gainesville: University Press of Florida, 2002.

Hammond, E. A. "The Spanish Fisheries of Charlotte Harbor." *Florida Historical Quarterly* 51 (1973): 355–80.

Hann, John H. "Cloak and Dagger in Apalachicole Province in Early 1686." *Florida Historical Quarterly* 78 (1999): 74–93.

———. "Late Seventeenth-Century Forebears of the Lower Creeks and Seminoles." *Southeastern Archaeology* 15 (1996): 66–80.

———. *Missions to the Calusa*. Introduction by W. H. Marquardt, translations by John H. Hann. Gainesville: University Press of Florida, 1991.

Howard, Rosalyn. *Black Seminoles in the Bahamas*. Gainesville: University Press of Florida, 2002.

Interviews of Seminole and Miccosukee people for interactive exhibit, Hall of South Florida People and Environments, Florida Museum of Natural History, Gainesville, 2000.

Jaap, Walter C., and Pamela Hallock. "Coral Reefs." In *Ecosystems of Florida*, edited by Ronald L. Myers and John J. Ewel, 574–616. Orlando: University of Central Florida Press, 1990.

Jepson, Michael. Personal Communication, based on oral history interview with Thomas R. "Blue" Fulford, 1995.

Judd, Alan. "Florida's Water Systematically Mismanaged." *Gainesville Sun*, vol. 115, no. 240, 1A, 4A, March 3, 1991.

———. "In Oregon, Water Comes First." *Gainesville Sun*, vol. 115, no. 244, pp. 1A, 8A-9A, March 7, 1991.

———. "Loopholes, or Reforms, Drain Taxes." *Gainesville Sun*, vol. 115, no. 348, pp. 1A, 7A, June 19, 1991.

Kozuch, Laura. *Sharks and Shark Products in Prehistoric South Florida*. Monograph 2. Gainesville: University of Florida, Institute of Archaeology and Paleoenvironmental Studies, 1993.

Lawson, Sarah, ed. and trans. *A Foothold in Florida: The Eye-Witness Account of Four Voyages Made by the French to That Region and Their Attempt at Colonisation, 1562–1568*. West Sussex, England: Antique Atlas Publications, 1992.

Livingstone, Robert J. "Inshore Marine Habitats." In *Ecosystems of Florida*, edited by Ronald L. Myers and John J. Ewel, 549–73. Orlando: University of Central Florida Press, 1990.

Luer, George M. "Calusa Canals in Southwestern Florida: Routes of Tribute and Exchange." *Florida Anthropologist* 42 (1989): 89–130.

Luer, George M., and Ryan J. Wheeler. "How the Pine Island Canal Worked: Topography, Hydraulics, and Engineering." *Florida Anthropologist* 50 (1997): 115–31.

Lyon, Eugene. *The Enterprise of Florida: Pedro Menéndez de Avilés and the Spanish Conquest of 1565–1568*. 1976. Reprint, Gainesville: University Press of Florida, 1983.

Mahon, John K. "The First Seminole War, November 21, 1817–May 24, 1818." *Florida Historical Quarterly* 77 (1998): 62–67.

———. *History of the Second Seminole War, 1835–1842*. Rev. ed. Gainesville: University Presses of Florida, 1985.

Marquardt, William H. "The Calusa Social Formation in Protohistoric South Florida." In *Power Relations and State Formation*, edited by T. C. Patterson and C. W. Gailey, 98–116. Washington, D.C.: Archeology Section, American Anthropological Association, 1987.

———. "The Emergence and Demise of the Calusa." In *Societies in Eclipse: Archaeology of the Eastern Woodlands Indians, a.d. 1400–1700*, edited by D. Brose, C. W. Cowan, and R. Mainfort, 157–71. Washington, D.C.: Smithsonian Institution Press, 2001.

———. "Four Discoveries: Environmental Archaeology in Southwest Florida." In *Case Studies in Environmental Archaeology*, edited by E. J. Reitz, L. A. Newsom, and S. J. Scudder, 17–32. New York: Plenum Press, 1996.

———. "Politics and Production among the Calusa of South Florida." In *Hunters and Gatherers*, volume 1, *History, Evolution, and Social Change*, edited by T. Ingold, D. Riches, and J. Woodburn, 161–88. London: Berg Publishers, 1988.

———, ed. *The Archaeology of Useppa Island*. Monograph 3. Gainesville: University of Florida, Institute of Archaeology and Paleoenvironmental Studies, 1999.

———, ed. *Culture and Environment in the Domain of the Calusa*. Monograph 1. Gainesville: University of Florida, Institute of Archaeology and Paleoenvironmental Studies, 1992.

Marquardt, William H., and Karen J. Walker. "Pineland: A Coastal Wet Site in Southwest

Florida." In *Enduring Records: The Environmental and Cultural Heritage of Wetlands*, edited by B. Purdy, 48–60. London: Oxbow Books, 2001.

Marsh, G. Alex, and Leni L. Bane. *Life along the Mangrove Shore*. Hobe Sound: Florida Classics Library, 1995.

McGoun, William E. *Prehistoric Peoples of South Florida*. Tuscaloosa: University of Alabama Press, 1993.

Miccosukee Tribe of Indians of Florida. "The Miccosukee Tribe Home Page: History." <www.miccosukeetribe.com/history.html> (accessed January 31, 2001).

Milanich, Jerald T. *Archaeology of Precolumbian Florida*. Gainesville: University Press of Florida, 1994.

———. *Florida Indians and the Invasion from Europe*. Gainesville: University Press of Florida, 1995.

———. *Laboring in the Fields of the Lord: Spanish Missions and Southeastern Indians*. Washington, D.C.: Smithsonian Institution Press, 1999.

Milanich, Jerald T., and Nara B. Milanich. "Revisiting the Freducci Map: A Description of Juan Ponce de León's 1513 Florida Voyage?" *Florida Historical Quarterly* 74 (1996): 319–28.

Montague, Clay L., and Richard G. Wiegert. "Salt Marshes." In *Ecosystems of Florida*, edited by Ronald L. Myers and John J. Ewel, 481–516. Orlando: University of Central Florida Press, 1990.

Myers, Ronald L., and John J. Ewel, eds. *Ecosystems of Florida*. Orlando: University of Central Florida Press, 1990.

Odum, Howard T., Elisabeth C. Odum, and Mark T. Brown. *Environment and Society in Florida*. Boca Raton, Fla.: Lewis Publishers, 1998.

Odum, William E., and Carole C. McIvor. "Mangroves." In *Ecosystems of Florida*, edited by Ronald L. Myers and John J. Ewel, 517–48. Orlando: University of Central Florida Press, 1990.

Porter, Kenneth W. *The Black Seminoles*. Gainesville: University Press of Florida, 1996.

Randazzo, Anthony F., and Douglas S. Jones. *The Geology of Florida*. Gainesville: University Press of Florida, 1997.

Rolle, Denys. *The Humble Petition of Denys Rolle*. Gainesville: University Presses of Florida, 1977.

Rudloe, Jack. *The Erotic Ocean*. New York: World Publishing Company, 1971.

———. *The Living Dock at Panacea*. New York: Alfred A. Knopf, 1977.

Ruppert, Edward E., and Richard S. Fox. *Seashore Animals of the Southeast*. Columbia: University of South Carolina Press, 1988.

Russo, Michael. "Why We Don't Believe in Archaic Ceremonial Mounds and Why We Should: The Case from Florida." *Southeastern Archaeology* 13 (1994): 93–109.

Sauer, Carl Ortwin. *The Early Spanish Main*. Berkeley: University of California Press, 1966.

Sears, William H. *Fort Center: An Archaeological Site in the Lake Okeechobee Basin*. Gainesville: University Press of Florida, 1982.

Seminole Tribe of Florida. "The Seminole Tribe of Florida: History." <www.seminoletribe.com/history/index.shtml> (accessed January 31, 2001).

Simons, M. H. "Shell-heaps of Charlotte Harbor, Florida." Smithsonian Institution, Annual Report for 1882, Papers Relating to Anthropology, pp. 794-96. Washington, D.C.

Solís de Merás, Gonzalo. *Pedro Menéndez de Avilés, Adelantado, Governor, and Captain-General of Florida: Memorial.* Facsimile reproduction of 1570 edition. Gainesville: University of Florida Press, 1964.

Sturtevant, William T. "Chakaika and the Spanish Indians: Documentary Sources Compared with Seminole Traditions." *Tequesta* 13 (1953): 35–73.

Suttles, Wayne, ed. *Handbook of North American Indians.* Volume 7, *Northwest Coast.* Washington, D.C.: Smithsonian Institution, 1990.

Swanton, John R. *Early History of the Creek Indians and Their Neighbors.* 1922. Reprint, Gainesville: University Press of Florida, 1998.

———. *The Indians of the Southeastern United States.* Smithsonian Institution, Bureau of American Ethnology, Bulletin 137. Washington, D.C.: U.S. Government Printing Office, 1946.

Voss, Gilbert L. *Coral Reefs of Florida.* Sarasota, Fla.: Pineapple Press, 1988.

Walker, Karen J. "The Material Culture of Precolumbian Fishing: Artifacts and Fish Remains from Coastal Southwest Florida." *Southeastern Archaeology* 19 (2000): 24–45.

Walker, Karen J., and William H. Marquardt, eds. *The Archaeology of Pineland: A Coastal Southwest Florida Village Complex, a.d. 50–1700.* Monograph 4. Gainesville: University of Florida, Institute of Archaeology and Paleoenvironmental Studies, 2005.

Walker, Karen J., Frank W. Stapor Jr., and William H. Marquardt. "Archaeological Evidence for a 1750–1450 BP Higher-Than-Present Sea Level along Florida's Gulf Coast." In *Holocene Cycles: Climate, Sea Levels, and Sedimentation,* edited by C. W. Finkl Jr., 205–18. *Journal of Coastal Research,* Special Issue 17, 1995.

Weddle, R. S. *Spanish Sea: The Gulf of Mexico in North American Discovery.* College Station: Texas A&M University Press, 1985.

Weisman, Brent R. *Like Beads on a String: A Cultural History of the Seminole Indians in North Peninsular Florida.* Tuscaloosa: University of Alabama Press, 1989.

———. *Unconquered People: Florida's Seminole and Miccosukee Indians.* Gainesville: University Press of Florida, 1999.

Wheeler, Ryan J. *Treasure of the Calusa: The Johnson/Willcox Collection.* Monographs in Florida Archaeology 1. Tallahassee: Rose Printing, 2000.

Widmer, Randolph J. *The Evolution of the Calusa: A Non-agricultural Chiefdom on the Southwest Florida Coast.* Tuscaloosa: University of Alabama Press, 1988.

Williams, John Lee. *The Territory of Florida: Or, Sketches of the Topography, Civil and Natural History of the Country, Its Climate, and the Indian Tribes from the First Discovery to the Present Time.* Facsimile of the original 1837 edition. Gainesville: University of Florida Press, 1962.

Worth, John E. "Fontaneda Revisited: Five Descriptions of Sixteenth-Century Florida." *Florida Historical Quarterly* 73 (1995): 339–52.

Index

Italics indicate an illustration or table.

Darcie A. MacMahon is assistant director for exhibits at the Florida Museum of Natural History, located at the University of Florida, Gainesville. For the past twenty-five years she has worked as an archaeologist and a museum professional. Her work currently focuses on public exhibitions, and she was project director of the museum's permanent exhibit, the Hall of South Florida People and Environments.

William H. Marquardt is curator in archaeology at the Florida Museum of Natural History, University of Florida, Gainesville. Since 1983 he has specialized in the archaeology of southwest Florida and has been instrumental in the establishment of the Randell Research Center at Pineland, a facility dedicated to research and public education. He was curator of the museum's permanent exhibit, the Hall of South Florida People and Environments.

Native Peoples, Cultures, and Places of the Southeastern United States

Edited by Jerald T. Milanich

The Apalachee Indians and Mission San Luis, by John H. Hann and Bonnie G. McEwan (1998)

Florida's Indians from Ancient Times to the Present, by Jerald T. Milanich (1998)

Unconquered People: Florida's Seminole and Miccosukee Indians, by Brent R. Weisman (1999)

The Ancient Mounds of Poverty Point: Place of Rings, by Jon L. Gibson (2000)

Before and After Jamestown: Virginia's Powhatans and Their Predecessors, by Helen C. Rountree and E. Randolph Turner (2002)

Ancient Miamians: The Tequesta of South Florida, by William E. McGoun (2002)

The Archaeology and History of the Native Georgia Tribes, by Max E. White (2002)

The Calusa and Their Legacy: South Florida People and Their Environments, by Darcie A. MacMahon and William H. Marquardt (2004)